WOMEN WHO ROCK 2

More Inspirational Stories of Success by Extraordinary Women

NATASHA DUSWALT

HYBRID GLOBAL PUBLISHING

Published by
Hybrid Global Publishing
301 E 57th Street, 4th Floor
New York, NY 10022

Manufactured in the United States of America, or in the United Kingdom when distributed elsewhere.

ISBN: 978-1-948181-00-6 (softcover)
ISBN: 978 1-948181-01-3 (e-book)

Cover design: Joe Potter
Copyediting and typesetting: Claudia Volkman

Disclaimer: The purpose of the book is to educate and entertain. The authors or publisher does not guarantee that anyone following the techniques, suggestions, tips, ideas, or strategies will become successful. The authors and publisher shall have neither liability or responsibility to anyone with respect to any loss or damage caused, or alleged to be caused, directly or indirectly by the information contained in this book.

www.NatashaDuswalt.com
www.PeakModels.com

AUTHOR PHOTOGRAPHERS

Natasha Duswalt — Val Westover
Sam Sorbo — Christopher Ameruoso
Donna Feldman — Nuru Kimondo
Cynthia Kersey — Maria Rangal
Cheri Tree — Walter Johnson
Tanya Brown — Val Westover Photography
Lynn Rose — Jerry Metellus
Nancy Matthews — Carlos Aristizabal
Lisa Reed — Shade Reed
Tesy Ward — John D. Ward
Melody Keymer Harper — Val Westover
Linda Kruse — Cutter Cutshaw
Gale Barbe — Val Westover
Michelle Calloway — StudioBooth
Judy Cook, MD — Val Westover
Kerri Courtright — Tom Stephenson
Dr. Haleh Damavandi — N/A
Lorna Day — Maria Miliotis
Susan DeRobertis — Tracy Rasinski
Giovanna Dottore — Teri Weber
Vivian R. England — N/A
Linda Fostek — Christina Stuart
Patricia Karen Gagic — Kyle Andrew Skinner
Mary Anne Kurzen — William Edwards Photography
Linnaea Mallette — Circe Denyer
Sue Mandell — Orletha Anderson
Sue Marting — N/A
Carey McLean — Val Westover
Joanne Neweduk — Jana Miko
Dr. Aurora Ongaro — Avonlea Photography Studio
Roberta Perry — N/A
Luz Sanchez — Elizabeth Gilbert
Merle M. Singer — David La Porte
Karen Strauss — Stephanie Adriana Westover
Shawna Swiger — Charr Crail
Bonnie Taub — N/A

DEDICATION

This book is dedicated to my true loves…
Craig, Tyler, Ryan and Hayden.
To my parents and grandparents who gave me my foundation.
To my sister Tania, brother Alex, Cameron, Cory, Tricia, Ron.
To Anne and Anton Duswalt, Pamela, William,
Courtney, Ashley, Taylor, Michael.
Thank you for lighting up my life!

This book is for those who live their lives
in pursuit of a higher purpose.

To those that realize that there is greatness
within each and every person.

Your life is a masterpiece—now go out
and make that your reality!

CONTENTS

Introduction

Women Who Rock 2 is another collection of stories gathered from women from all walks of life. Each author who shares her story also reveals her unique female experience. We as the readers are pulled into their lives with a new appreciation and understanding of their journey.

With every story we can all find ourselves in a version of each author. The stories differ, the settings differ, but the need for the human spirit to triumph comes through loud and clear.

There is an unseen thread that within each story is the need and desire to move forward while taking along the lessons learned and insights gained. *Women Who Rock 2* sets the stage for women all over the world to look within and find their inner strength to live out their destiny. The purpose of this book is to lift others and show what is possible. Every author in this book started somewhere and has created a life of purpose. When one succeeds it gives everyone else the chance to succeed as well.

Women have the unique ability to bring life into the world, and with that honor comes great responsibility. I am honored at the thought of the lives this book will touch. I am honored to know that with every woman who decides to live the best version of herself, there will be an unseen positive reaction in her home, her life, and her community.

Every woman who has the courage to light the way for others is also lighting the way for future generations beyond her lifetime.

Natasha Duswalt
Women Who Rock 2

THOUGHTS AND WORDS

Natasha Duswalt

Our thoughts and words are infinite in what they create and produce.

In my late twenties I attended a Tony Robbins seminar and I made a decision, formed out of a thought, backed with passion, and directed by a vision to own my own business.

I started modeling at the age of seventeen, and had traveled around the world and realized that I wanted something else, but the beliefs I had formed around my career were limiting my growth. Somewhere the lines were blurred and my personal value was based on how I looked, how my photos turned out, what size I was wearing and what clients I was booking. Don't get me wrong I had a great ride and I would not change it for the world. I loved the industry but wanted to have longevity. The trick was, what's the next step?

That question brought me to start Peak Models & Talent in Los Angeles. Even though my mind was riddled with doubt, I was able to apply all of the skills that I had picked up while modeling and parlayed that into a company where I am able to help others on a daily basis.

The thoughts and words we have behind the scenes of our lives need to be monitored in order to succeed.

To overcome fear and doubt my background mantra was to always be of service to anyone that I encountered. However, after many years I found that the responsibility of the agency was wearing me down, and I was about to face a new challenge that I certainly was not expecting . . . ever.

In October 2006 I was told by a doctor that I had Hodgkin's Lymphoma, a blood cancer. At that moment all I could think was, "What does this mean? Am I going to die? What will my children and husband do without me?" All of the thoughts came racing like a train through my head, unstoppable, fearful, terrifying, and completely unhappy thoughts. My reaction was tears. My tears were for the kids that I had brought into this world to take care of, tears for a husband that married me to have a family with, tears for me that I might have to knowingly go down a path that could possibly result in my mortal end. All of this was overwhelming and painful.

My thoughts were taking control of my existence. This is what happens when we face life on life's terms. After battling the thoughts of despair, I finally took control of my thoughts and words. Cancer might have sucker-punched me at first, but I needed to gain control of my thoughts.

Every day I started to focus on living. Living meant doing the things I wanted to do in-between doctor visits and treatments. Living meant envisioning myself with my kids and husband well after this part of my life was over. My choice was to see my life after cancer, not to stay in the fear. My life needed to be focused on faith. The faith that I could do this, and the faith that God was with me and wanted me to continue living.

Contrary to popular belief, I was not "fighting" cancer, I was surrendering control over to God because the idea of "fighting" cancer was too big of a battle to do alone.

The point is—that no matter what happens we get to take control of our thoughts and words. My diagnosis was just that—a diagnosis that just happened to require medical care.

I decided after surrendering, that this was nothing more than a small problem that would pass through my life, and that was it.

I stopped focusing on the negative and instead focused on the fact that this would soon be over.

When people asked about my illness I simply told that that I was "diagnosed," meaning that it was someone else's opinion that I was being treated for cancer—not mine.

Do you see how different that is?

Most people say they have cancer. I personally believe that this is not helpful. I never owned the "C" word.

After 12 rounds of chemo I was done with the process.

I have been called a survivor. That is one label. People also ask me if I'm in remission, but I believe remission implies that it is still possibly there. I prefer to say I was cured of a diagnosis back in 2006.

The rest is history. Life wants me back in full force, living a life of purpose . . . on purpose.

The thoughts and words you choose to use in your daily life are very powerful and with a few changes in your daily dialogue you will notice that you feel better every day. We all have those moments where we question everything.

When someone asks you how your day is going, think positive! If you are not in the hospital you are GREAT! The bottom line is that you get to choose the thoughts you think and the words you use, and it will feel much better to choose empowering words everywhere you go with every person you encounter.

Remember that everyone you meet is probably struggling with thoughts and feelings just as you are. Giving them something positive to think about or a kind word can really lift their spirits.

One of my favorite things to do is to ask them a question that might get them thinking of something wonderful they could be doing.

The power of thought is immeasurable. The power of our words and language shapes our feelings and outcomes as a person.

Everyone has a mind that is like a garden. Plant seeds of positive thought everywhere you go. Look for the good in every situation. I believe that every day that I am lucky enough to be here to help others, is a successful day.

My greatest personal success is realizing what empowers me, and what I am capable of accomplishing is infinite. I still have so much more to do and that is exactly why I was cured of my diagnosis in 2006.

Natasha Duswalt is an author, speaker and the president and founder of Peak Models & Talent in Los Angeles. As an international model, Natasha has had the rare opportunity to travel all over the world in places including New York, Miami, Hong Kong, Japan, Taiwan, Mexico and several other locations working with top designers and companies.

Natasha has been featured on numerous television shows including Baywatch *and* Growing Pains, *as well as the hit movie by Oliver Stone,* The Doors. *She was also hired as an ESPN Spokesmodel and has appeared on numerous television commercials.*

Peak Models & Talent has been touted as one of Los Angeles' top agencies, booking with high-end clients such as Guess, Forever 21, Six Flags Theme Parks, Kardashians, Kendall & Kylie, Intel, Nokia, Reebok, Disney, ABS Clothing, Skechers, Nike, Dell, Audi, Mercedes, Honda, Speedo, Tempurpedic Sleep Systems, Starbucks, Bebe, Wells Fargo, Honda, Patagonia, Princess Cruises, Tommy Bahama, Kmart, and Target, just to name a few.

Natasha, a proud cancer survivor, and currently lives in Los Angeles with her husband, Craig Duswalt, and their three boys.

www.PeakModels.com

LET THERE BE LIGHT

Sam Sorbo

"Kevin, I have an idea for a movie," I said, with both excitement and trepidation. It wasn't the first time I had had an idea to produce something, but ideas are worth only the paper they are printed on in Hollywood, which is to say, ideas are less than a dime a dozen.

A year before, there had been little hope of getting my faith-based television program on the air without a bona fide writer, but I remained undeterred. My drive stemmed from my aspiration to see morally principled entertainment on TV. A producer-contact introduced me to Dan Gordon, who had been the showrunner on Highway to Heaven with Michael Landon. He loved the idea—particularly the faith-based aspect of it—and decided to work on it with me.

Sadly, early in the very involved and frustratingly slow process of show development, circumstances dictated that Dan recuse himself from the project. Our friendship persevered despite that.

With our new writer, Kevin and I pitched Miracle Man fervently and sold it to NBC and Sony, but timing or politics or just plain nonsense moved it onto a shelf instead of into prime time.

My attitude at the time was that, although I had conceived an excellent idea for a show, I would not be showrunning or even writing on it. True, we needed someone with a proven track record to run the show, but this experience taught me the hard way that I should never cede my power so easily. At the time, though, I focused on my nationally syndicated daily radio show. I was stretched thin, and I considered myself a liability rather than an asset.

I was wrong.

About a year later, I was in my husband Kevin's small upstairs bedroom-office, sitting in the oversized, carved-wood antique chair I had bought in New Zealand, and telling him I had a new idea. The afternoon sun was streaming through the window, lighting up dust particles in the air.

"Tell me about it," he replied, turning his seat to face me, like a good, supportive husband.

I smiled. "The world's greatest atheist has a near-death experience that completely contradicts his disbelief, and he has to rethink his entire purpose in life."

Kevin seemed a bit stunned, and after a moment he said quietly, "Interesting. What are you going to do with it?"

"I want to write it as a script, obviously. You like it?"

"Of course I like it. It's got so much potential. I love it," he confessed easily.

"I need a writer, though. My name won't sell it. Plus, frankly I'm not that good."

"Sam, you're too modest. But if you want a writer, I have a few names you can call. What about that guy we had for *Miracle Man*? Dan Gordon?"

"Yeah, I'm going to reach out to him. I'm pumped!" I got up from the chair and stood in the doorway, giddy with the power that a new idea always evokes in me.

"Good! But, Sam, can you take this on, with everything else?"

"Aw, Kevy, if only I had the choice." I leaned over his desk as I spoke. "I'd sit back and eat bonbons all day long and read. But the way this idea just came to me . . . it was a gift from God obviously, and I am obliged to see it through." I puckered my lips for a peck. Kevin kissed me and smiled, looking in my eyes.

"OK," he said, laughing. "Keep me posted!"

I called Dan Gordon. A very accomplished Hollywood screenwriter, he wrote *The Hurricane* with Denzel Washington and *Wyatt Earp* for Kevin Costner.

"Hey, Dan, I've got an idea for a movie. Would you consider writing it with me?"

"No," he answered succinctly.

"Oh," I said, embarrassed. Of course, he wouldn't need anyone to collaborate with.

Then he continued, "But, Sam, we haven't seen each other for a while—let's have lunch."

Over lunch Dan regaled me with the story of the screenplay he had just sold for over $1.25 million. Toward the end of our lunch, Dan offered, "So, tell me your idea for a movie." I thought maybe he'd give me a tip or something.

I pitched the idea to him. He thought about it for a moment, then nodded and said, "I like it. We'll write it together."

Neither Kevin nor I believe in serendipity, or what some people call chance. Lady Luck, roll of the dice, karma—none of those are real. Things only appear to happen by chance because our perspective is too close to view the entire plan, until, fully executed, we stand back in awe and exclaim on its magnificence.

About two weeks after I began collaborating on the script with Dan, I had nearly finished writing the first draft.

Then, like a lightning bolt out of a clear blue sky, Kevin received a phone call from Sean Hannity.

They chatted briefly about golf and tennis, Sean's favorite sports, and then he cut to the chase. "You know, Kevin, I've been thinking of getting into movie production. It's a powerful medium, and you've got a great handle on it. What do you say? Do you have a faith-based project we could collaborate on?"

Later that afternoon, Kevin told me about the conversation. "That's my movie!" I squealed, jumping up and down.

A few weeks later Dan, Kevin, and I flew to New York City. For about half an hour we pitched the film to Sean, and he decided right then and there to fund the entire project.

Of course, there is a lot more to this story—hard work and tenacity and struggles— but suffice it to say that despite all the things that can go wrong in such a complicated and creative business, Let There Be Light is exactly the film I intended to make!

Launching the film on October 27, 2017, we held the second per-screen box office against Thor and stayed the course through a little competition called Star Wars. Our movie was the fourth-highest-grossing faith-based movie of 2017, and it's up for awards at the MovieGuide gala of 2018. Being appreciated by your peers is a wonderful thing, but even better are the countless emails I've received from viewers, who say the movie profoundly impacted them and changed their lives.

The lightbulb is a world-recognized symbol of an idea because light illuminates the darkness, revealing things previously unseen and clarifying confusion. Light attracts us, helps us, and even warms us. In the beginning of time, God said, "Let there be light."

Best. Idea. Ever.

Sam Sorbo studied biomedical engineering at Duke University before pursuing a career in entertainment. She is an award-winning actress, author, radio host, international model, and homeschooling mom to three children with Kevin Sorbo. Her book They're YOUR Kids: An Inspirational Journey from Self-Doubter to Home School Advocate *empowers parents to home educate, and she frequently speaks on education across the nation. She wrote a follow-up book called* Teach from Love: A School Year Devotional for Families *(Broadstreet Publishing).*

Sam co-wrote, produced, and co-starred in the 2017 feature film Let There Be Light *(executive producer, Sean Hannity; director, Kevin Sorbo). Her boys also acted in the film, making it truly a family affair. The award-winning film was the fourth-highest-grossing faith-based feature film of 2017, spawning a book version of the film and the devotional,* Share the Light.

www.SamSorbo.com

HOW I STARTED TO BELIEVE I WAS GOOD ENOUGH

Donna Feldman

It's just as important to work on your inner beauty as it is to work on your outer appearance, who other people perceive you to be. Think about the story you replay in your head. Is it actually real? Is it true? You can change your mind-set when you decide to change your story. This "story" I'm referring to has to do with the destructive beliefs you have about yourself.

My story used to be that I was such a shy girl growing up, and modeling was somewhat of a stage for me—a safe place to pretend that I was a powerful, sexy, confident woman. In my "real life," I was attached to the idea that I was still that shy, self-conscious girl who didn't feel quite sure of herself.

It didn't help that I chose a profession where you are judged on a daily basis. Your mind starts playing tricks on you, and you can't help but ask yourself, "Am I skinny enough, pretty enough, approachable enough? Are my teeth white enough, are my boobs perky enough, is my skin glowing enough, am I young enough?" The big question on a daily basis becomes, "Am I ENOUGH?"

I ended up getting invited to a weeklong Tony Robbins workshop, and it was a life changing experience. I learned a lot about dealing with personal relationships, career, family, and shaping my destiny in order to live a successful and fulfilling life. The most powerful and memorable thing I learned that week had to do with the importance of being grateful and having positive and inspiring thoughts running in my head rather than negative or self-destructive thoughts. As Tony Robbins said, "Change your story, change your life. Divorce the story of limitation and marry the story of the truth, and everything changes."

This was a huge reality check for me. I finally understood that if I wasn't that powerful, confident, sexy woman in my real life, how was I able to project it so well in front of the camera? The power was inside me all along.

Once that story shifted for me, I wasn't pretending anymore. I was so much freer and happier knowing that I was getting hired for so much more than just being a particular measurement or fitting into some unrealistic mold. I learned that surviving the modeling world is all about who you are, how you show up, your networking skills, your professionalism, your personality. I was finally able to just be myself and appreciate the qualities I have to offer, rather than focusing on imaginary flaws.

You can have an amazing breakthrough in your life once you change those limiting thoughts. I invite you to look deeply within yourself and ask, "What's my story? Is it beneficial in any way?" If not, what would you lose by changing it? Better yet, what would you gain?

Donna Feldman has been a true all-media modeling powerhouse for nearly fifteen years. Her statuesque 5'10" figure, flowing dark hair, sultry eyes, and exotic Mediterranean features are recognized by hundreds of millions of people across the globe, thanks to her countless magazine covers (GQ, Esquire, Maxim, FHM, to name a few), fashion editorials, high-profile ad campaigns, TV and film appearances, and her constant presence in some of the biggest entertainment websites in the world.

Donna got her break when she distracted the eyes of international TV viewers during the 2005 Academy Awards as the stunning hostess hired to escort Oscar winners across the stage. Amongst those watching were the producers of Fashion House, the Twentieth Television dramatic series starring Bo Derek. Donna was instantly cast in the recurrent role of Gloria, an unscrupulous temptress who uses her sex appeal to get her way. The show aired 6 nights a week on MyNetworkTV, in over 50 countries. Donna followed her TV breakthrough with a head-turning role on NBC's hit game show, Deal or No Deal, hosted by comedian Howie Mandel.

As a model, she graced the catwalks during Los Angeles' Mercedes Benz fashion week and at the biggest runway show on the West Coast, Macy's Passport. Her international print campaigns include Visa BlackCard, Bebe,Rampage, Jockey, Target, Revlon, Sean John, New Yorker (European retail chain), Biosilk, Jaguar, Fila, Wella, MiraclesuitSwimwear, Felina Lingerie, Pleasure State VIP lingerie (Australia), Verizon Wireless, Zanetti (Italy), Diesel ,Panasonic , as well as ads for Ceasar's Palace and Bellagio Resort and Casino in Las Vegas. Catalog clients include Quelle (Austria), Madeleine (Germany), Venus (US), and Apart (Europe). She has also been featured in popular TV commercials and chart-topping music videos.

THE GIFT OF GIVING:
WHY I HAVE BEEN CALLED TO SERVE

Cynthia Kersey

The story of an unstoppable woman!

Who knew that when my husband of twenty years and I separated in December 1999, my pain would open the door to my greatest purpose?

We had planned on spending the holidays with my parents in Florida. Now my son and I were going alone. I felt devastated and overwhelmed, but somehow in the midst of my pain, I made a promise to myself that the next Christmas would not find me at my parents' house feeling sorry for myself. I would instead dedicate myself to doing something for someone else.

As soon as I got home, I called my mentor and friend Millard Fuller, the founder of Habitat for Humanity International, asking him for advice. I met him while interviewing him for my first book, *Unstoppable*. He said "Cynthia, when you have a great pain in your life, you need a greater purpose." He told me about his recent visit to Nepal, one of the poorest nations in the world, and suggested that building a house for a Nepalese family in need could be a great project for me.

As I sat with his suggestion, I thought, How many houses would I need to build that would be bigger than this pain in my life? Even though I had never built one house in my life, it wasn't until I got to the number of 100 houses that felt bigger than my pain.

That was a crazy, audacious goal, and I had no idea how I would make it happen! Each house would cost $2,000. I was a single mom, living on the proceeds from a $14.95 book. I had no big community of potential donors to draw from, and I didn't even know exactly where Nepal was! But I had a purpose that was bigger than my pain and was invigorated by my newfound project. Plus I was grateful to have something to take my mind off of myself and my problems.

Throughout that year of grieving the loss of my marriage, there were times when I felt so depressed that I didn't even want to get out of bed. When that happened, I'd think about the Nepalese families who didn't even have a decent place to sleep at night. That thought got me up and moving forward.

One year after separating from my husband and my subsequent phone call to Millard, I had reached my goal of raising $200,000 simply by asking everyone I came in contact with to donate. I brought a team of 18 people to Nepal over the New Year's holiday, and we built the first three of the 100 houses that would subsequently be built over the following year.

I'll never forget the connection I formed with one of the women who received a home we funded. Chandra was also a single woman; she was supporting seven family members including her parents, brothers, and sisters. They all lived together in a tiny one-bedroom shack.

Although Chandra had diligently saved money each week for 18 years from her job at a biscuit factory, she would never have been able to save enough money to build a home without the help of our project. Her gratitude was apparent in her constant smile. Even though we didn't speak the same language, our hearts were connected. When it was time for me to leave, both of us were in tears, and she begged me to never forget her. As we hugged good-bye, I thought, *Forget you? How could I ever forget you? You were the purpose that got me through the most difficult year of my life!*

That experience changed my life forever. It was the first time I had really experienced the transformational power of giving. When I started this project, I thought I was doing something great for these families. What I hadn't expected was how this project would change my life!

I also experienced something else first hand: the law of giving and receiving. Unexpectedly, that year I earned more money speaking and selling my $14.95 book than I had earned in a very successful corporate sales career earning a six-figure income. I was starting to understand the spiritual axiom, "Give, and it shall be given unto you." The Scripture doesn't say *wait* until you get something, whether it's more money, more time, more love, more support, or more resources. It says give.

The law of receiving is activated by giving. When we wait for something in the future to change before we give, it puts us in a congested state. Stopping the circulation of giving is like stopping the flow of blood. Whenever blood stops flowing, our cells begin to die and our body ceases to function.

I began to see how, when we give, we become a channel for the universe to work through. And this channel is activated through giving. That experience fundamentally changed how I lived and ran my business. With every new book or project that I launched, I attached a philanthropic project to each one. This ignited a deep passion in my heart and brought great joy and meaning to my business.

In 2005 my second book, *Unstoppable Women*, came out, and I was looking for my next philanthropic project. I received an invitation "out of the blue" to attend the first ever Rural African Women's Conference. The only thing I knew about this conference was that women from rural Kenya were going to meet with us and share their story. While my schedule was full, I knew I needed to say yes. So I booked my flight and flew half way around the world.

Forty other women from North America said yes, and we all flew to the Nairobi airport for the next step of our journey.

Picture this: We're on a crowded, uncomfortable bus, and the shock absorbers are definitely not working. What's worse, it's hot and muggy and I am crammed on a bus with women I didn't even know ten minutes before. Now it's been 12 *l-o-n-g* hours. With each bump in the road, my body was increasingly more uncomfortable and I was getting crankier by the minute.

In desperation I prayed, "God, please help me get over my little self so that I don't miss why I was called to fly halfway around the world."

An hour later we drove around a corner, and I could see our destination in the distance. It was a very modest college campus where the women's conference was going to be held. There were a couple hundred women standing in the driveway, and as we got closer, I could see them smiling and waving. I thought, *Wow, they must be here for us!*

As I walked off the bus, a woman took my hand and pulled me into the middle of this large group of women and we all began singing and dancing. It was as if the last 12 hours disappeared. I was in heaven!

The next morning at 8:00 a.m. I walked into the auditorium and saw four hundred women waiting to take the stage. I found out later that many of the women had never left their small village before in their life and yet they had walked miles, many of them days, to meet with me and the forty other *mzungas* ("white people").

Over the next five days, each woman stood up and, through an interpreter, told their heart-wrenching story. The first woman shared how her youngest daughter got malaria and the nearest medical clinic was twenty miles away. She carried her daughter for a full day, and before she reached the clinic, her daughter died in her arms. And what made her death even more heartbreaking is that she could have been saved with medicine costing about $3, the price of a cup of coffee.

The next woman told us that she and her eight-year-old daughter spend four to six hours every day fetching water and firewood to keep their family alive. That didn't leave them any time to do more productive things like attend school or allow the mom to earn an income to adequately care for her family.

The third woman told us that her family frequently goes without food for days because they have no way to preserve fruits and vegetables, and it's even worse in times of drought.

Their greatest hope and concern was how they could make sure their children got an education. Because without it, they said, "nothing will ever change." These women weren't there to complain. They were looking for solutions to create a better life for their children and their families.

And as I listened to story after story, I first felt sadness and great compassion for things they had to endure that I couldn't even imagine. Then I started to feel outrage that simply by virtue of where they were born meant they'd have to live a life of backbreaking poverty, with little way out.

A voice in my head, as clear as a bell, said, "Cynthia, you've got to do something about this!" And immediately I heard another, even louder voice that said, "Don't even think about it! This problem is so big and has been going on for so long. What difference could you really make?" Feeling overwhelmed, I decided to ignore both voices and just be present to the experience I was having.

Five days later, it was time to get back on that bus. As we were saying our good-byes, hugging these women I have since fallen in love with, they were pleading with me about something, but I didn't understand. I turned to my interpreter, and he told me, "They're saying, 'Please don't forget us.'"

Something welled up inside of me, and I couldn't ignore their pleas, so I promised them that I would do something to help them.

This time, riding the bus for twelve hours, my mind was racing. *What am I going to do about this? . . . Cynthia, you made this promise, but where do you even start?*

I visited my friend Debbie Ford over Thanksgiving, and she told me that her son Beau did the most wonderful thing for his bar mitzvah. Instead of getting a bunch of gifts or cash, he wanted to do something meaningful and asked people to donate money to build a school in Uganda.

It was as if the lightbulb came on. I knew at that moment what I was going to do to make good on the promise I made to those women.

I was turning fifty in a few months, and I decided I would make that birthday something meaningful by having a party and turning it into a fund-raiser. I wanted to build a school in East Africa just like Beau had done.

We booked the Shangai Reds Restaurant in Marina Del Rey, California, and I invited all of my friends to attend. But I gave them a specific request. Instead of giving me a present, I wanted their help to give children in East Africa a present—the gift of an education.

One hundred people attended my party, and it was standing room only. And something happened that I hadn't anticipated. People were coming up and thanking me! It wasn't the typical "thank you for having a great party." They were thanking me for giving them the opportunity to make a difference—to be able to contribute to something that would forever change the lives of hundreds of children around the world.

That night we raised $80,000. I thought, *If I could do this in one night, what could I do if I really put my time and energy into it?*

Suddenly I knew what I could to do to keep my promise to these women in a much bigger way. I started the Unstoppable Foundation, and I got serious. I did some research and *I discovered something that shocked me.*

There were many well-intended organizations building schools in developing countries. But unfortunately many of those schools were sitting empty.

Why were they empty?

Because you can build a school . . . but if girls don't have access to clean water, they spend hours every day fetching water and aren't able to attend school.

You can build a school . . . but if children don't have access to basic medical treatment, they're often sick and can't attend school.

You can build a school . . . but If children don't have nutritious food, they're hungry and malnourished.

You can build a school . . . but if the parents can't generate an income, how can the project sustain itself?

It can't!

I had an epiphany.

If this is going to work, we don't just need a school. We need to also provide the kids with access to 2) clean water; 3) healthcare; 4) nutritious food; and 5) training for the parents to earn an income so the entire project is self-sustaining.

That became my marching orders to find an organization that would be able to implement all five pillars. I was fortunate to find a partner on the ground in Kenya, We Charity, who was implementing all five of these services. As a result of that partnership, the Unstoppable Foundation created a program called Sponsor a Village.

It's not charity in the traditional sense. It's empowerment!

I began asking people to join me in this vision. And what I discovered is that people really care. They care about others—whether those in their own communities or halfway around the world.

And so they gave. They had fund-raisers. Their children had fund-raisers. They asked their friends and community to write checks. They gave up their birthday parties.

And the results have been amazing.

Because of our generous supporters, we have educated over 35,000 children and impacted over 75,000 men, women, and children in the Maasai Mara alone with our five-pillar model, and we have now expanded to India.

Entire communities are now thriving with the tools to lift themselves out of poverty.

I would never have imagined that the choice I made in 1999 to find a purpose that was bigger than my pain would have been the doorway to a whole new life that would shape my destiny forever.

It's brought me indescribable joy, meaning, and satisfaction.

As my mentor, Millard Fuller always said, "I feel like the richest person on the planet."

Cynthia Kersey is the founder and CEO of the Unstoppable® Foundation, whose focus is to ensure that every child on the planet has access to the life-long gift of education.

She is a respected leader in the transformational industry, a best-selling author of two books, Unstoppable *and* Unstoppable Women, *and an international speaker.*

Cynthia knows first-hand that giving is not only good for business, it's good for the soul.

Cynthia inspires people to give and provides business professionals with a practical action plan on how they can expand their business, create customer evangelists, and become completely invigorated about their life and business by integrating generosity as a fundamental part of their business model.

Cynthia embodies her message and has integrated giving and contribution into her life and business for well over two decades. The Unstoppable Foundation has provided a daily education to over 35,000 children, and it provides access to life-saving services such as clean water, healthcare, and nutritious food through organic gardens to over 75,000 men, women and children in Kenya alone!

UnstoppableFoundation.org

TAKE IT TO THE BANK

Cheri Tree

When it comes to being a business owner, entrepreneur, or sales professional, you're likely either winning the proverbial numbers game or losing it. Let's face it, you're either really good at sales, or you just suck at selling! For me, I sucked—and this is where my story begins . . .

I started off at the bottom . . . the very bottom! My dream of being a successful entrepreneur got crushed when I realized that I sucked at sales. I was so terrible that during my entire first year in sales as a commission-only part-time financial advisor I only earned $700.

I was the worst salesperson on the team! For five years, I studied every sales training program I could get my hands on. I read dozens of books, listened to audios, watched webinars, attended seminars—all to no avail. I even hired coaches and mentors and paid them thousands of dollars (money I didn't have), and still nothing made a significant difference. I got my income up to $72,000, but I had accumulated over $30,000 in credit card debt and still felt like I was going backwards. I felt like throwing in the towel and giving up, but I was too stubborn to quit!

Then suddenly the game changed. I discovered a missing link in the sales process and cracked the code to making millions of dollars. The next thing I knew, I was winning trips, achieving record sales, earning an incredible income, and being featured on magazine covers! I went from zero to hero overnight—and everyone wanted to know my secret.

As a result of using my secret weapon, B.A.N.K., I was able to take my annual income from $72,000 to over $1 million within three years. I hit sales records that have never been hit before—and have never been broken since—when I took my income from $8,000 per month to more than $261,000 per month in twenty-eight days! The B.A.N.K. system supercharged my sales in a way that made me feel like I was a superhero, and the rest, as they say, is history!

You may be asking, "What is B.A.N.K.?" B.A.N.K. is personality-based, people-focused, and profit-driven. It is the only methodology in the world scientifically validated to predict buying behavior in less than ninety seconds. It was my way of winning the numbers game and getting way more yeses and converting more sales than ever before.

This book is filled with amazing success stories, and I'm grateful to contribute my own. My story is not just about my massive success. It's also about my massive failures, how I overcame monumental adversity, and how you can too.

Once I started using the B.A.N.K. methodology and experiencing such fantastic results, I couldn't keep it a secret any longer. I started training every sales team member who was part of my network. I wanted everyone to experience the benefits I was experiencing. If B.A.N.K. was really that big of a game-changer, the world deserved to know about it.

However, my success was envied, and I reached a place where I was limited in my ability to train other people because of corporate politics. I was faced with a major decision. Was I more about the money or integrity? As enticing as the fame and fortune was, I chose to stand up for what I believe in and put people before profits rather than vice versa.

I resigned from the company I was working for on August 8, 2008. I then chose to start my own training company, BANKCODE, where I could share my game-changing methodology with the world. I didn't want to be limited or restricted in any way from sharing something that could change others' lives. I knew the pain of rejection and the agony of defeat intimately. I wanted to bring my vision and my mission to the world, and I wanted to make a difference, not just a dollar.

As a result, I walked away from nearly $2 million a year. My income went to zero overnight. With my entrepreneurial spirit, I expected I could climb back up that mountain.

Unfortunately I was immediately met with significant adversity. The company I resigned from sued me within ten days of my resignation, attempting to stop me from growing my

own business. Unwilling to be bullied, I used every resource I had and fought it all the way through federal court. This was one of the worst battles of my life, and although I won the right to run my own business, I still lost everything.

Just like a perfect storm, 2008 also marked the collapse of a good portion of the entire American economy. I had about $8 million in real estate holdings at the time, and my portfolio became worth nothing practically overnight. My cash flow situation went to a negative $60,000 per month, and in the blink of an eye, I was broke. Everything I'd been accumulating my entire life—my homes, my cars, my investments—disappeared before my eyes.

With all of my real estate foreclosed, I took all that I had left and loaded up five different storage units. Shortly thereafter, the storage unit company called me and said, "Cheri, your stuff is about to go to auction if we don't receive a payment." I was drowning in my own failure!

Now, because my whole financial life had crumbled, I was forced to the inevitable: filing Chapter 7 bankruptcy. Again, in a moment, everything I had was gone. I had no credit. I had to give up my homes. I had to give up my cars. I did keep one car, but a tow truck company came out in the middle of the night looking for it. I couldn't handle the stress anymore, so I just turned it in. I literally had nothing left to my name.

Being a resourceful entrepreneur, I decided that rather than having my stuff go up for auction, I would find a better, cheaper solution. Soon I found a 1,600-square-foot storage unit in Newport Beach, California. It was a huge warehouse, with a roll-up door and enough room to store all of my belongings.

Coincidentally, at the back of the storage unit was a tiny set of wooden steps that went up to a small loft, maybe around 150 or 200 square feet. In that moment, I suddenly had an idea: "What if I could actually move in here and make this my home?" This would allow me to save money so I could rebuild my training company.

Around the same time, I was asked by a good friend to speak at his company's market launch event. It wasn't a paid speaking gig, but it gave my new little training company some exposure.

I needed any break I could get! After I trained the entire sales force about B.A.N.K., I received a standing ovation. Everyone wanted to buy the program. Unfortunately, I didn't have anything for sale. I hadn't developed it into a product at that point. It was more of a concept that I taught.

As I left the stage, a gentleman chased after me. "Cheri, that's one of the best sales training programs I've ever seen. I want to help you turn it into a tangible product, as long as you're willing to pay for it."

Well, this was the break I was looking for, except that I didn't have the money to pay for it, and I didn't have the credit either. But I don't accept defeat, and failure is never an option. My mom always taught me, "Where there's a will, there's a way." Now I knew it was the right thing for me to move into that storage unit.

Life in a storage unit is an interesting story by itself. It was a huge warehouse in an industrial park, with florescent lights and no running water.

Luckily I was a trained whitewater rafting guide and had taken a course on wilderness survival. I went down to the local camping supply store and bought a five-gallon bucket called a Luggable Loo. That five-gallon bucket came with a toilet seat, so I made that my bathroom for the next eighteen months. I bought a membership at the gym so I could shower. Some days I never made it to the gym, so I either didn't shower or just rinsed my head under the water spigot outside the building. It was a crazy time, not that long ago. If we ever have the opportunity to meet, I can tell you some pretty funny stories . . . and some not-so-funny stories too.

Most importantly, what I want to share with you is that we all have adversity. Some of us have more, and some have less. But we all have it. And that's how I know we can overcome it. I rebuilt my entire life from that place!

It was there, in that little creepy storage unit, that I took my decade of experience with B.A.N.K. and not only turned it into a revolutionary product but also built the foundation for a company that's now all over the world in more than forty different countries.

I could tell you story after story about the adversity I faced during that time. The key for me was that failure was never an option. Quitting was never an option. I was committed—no matter what—whatever it took! This is what it means to be a ROCKSTAR!

The best thing that ever happened to me was losing everything. Living in that storage unit for eighteen months erased my attachment to money. I had made millions of dollars, but now I was no longer attached to money; instead, I grew my attachment to people and purpose.

B.A.N.K. has completely changed my heart from the inside out. It's not greed and success that's driving me—it's seeing the lives of every single person who gets in contact with B.A.N.K.'s incredible message change in the blink of an eye. That's why Les Brown proudly declared that "B.A.N.K. is a game changer for every entrepreneur and sales professional."

Self-esteem increases when you win, not when you lose. Unfortunately the world is set up to make you fail. To be a ROCKSTAR, you need to be willing to fail over and over again, and still get back up and fight for your dreams.

My dream goes far beyond helping people win the sales game. I actually want to change the world! My mission is to create "one world, one language." We live on a planet with seven billion people. More than 6,500 different languages are spoken on earth, but there's only one language that I believe unites the entire human race. That is B.A.N.K., the language of people.

I believe one idea can change the world. My idea is called B.A.N.K. It has changed my life and has allowed me to live my ultimate ROCKSTAR life—and you can take that to the bank!

Want to know your B.A.N.K. code? Go to mybankcode.com/rockstar and crack your code! Use the access code Rockstar to get your custom B.A.N.K. Code Personality Report for free (save $97).

Cheri Tree is a successful entrepreneur, professional keynote speaker, world-renowned sales trainer, best-selling author, and executive business coach. She is the founder and CEO of BANKCODE, with clients in more than forty countries worldwide. Cheri has spoken to hundreds of thousands of entrepreneurs and sales professionals globally and has been featured in numerous international publications, sharing the stage with icons such as Tony Robbins, Robert Kiyosaki, Suze Orman, and Sir Richard Branson.

Cheri has also lectured at Harvard University and the University of California at Berkeley and is considered the number-one personality-based sales trainer in the world. Her expertise earned her the American Riviera Woman Entrepreneur of the Year Award, and she's been nominated for the Women in Business Award and Innovator of the Year Award by the Orange County Business Journal. In order to teach B.A.N.K. to anyone who wants to learn, Cheri wrote her groundbreaking book Why They Buy *(whytheybuy.com). When not traveling the world to share B.A.N.K., Cheri lives with her beautiful family in Laguna Beach, California.*

www.bankcode.com

FINDING PEACE AMID THE CHAOS

Tanya Brown

Success, to me, means overcoming major adversities in my life. I am the youngest sister of the late Nicole Brown Simpson. But what people don't know about me is that I have survived depression and an attempted suicide—all from unresolved stress, chaos, grief, and pain.

Tragedy began for me when I was a teenager. I had to bury six friends in high school. We did not have the counselors kids have today. So I stuffed my feelings. Little would I know, this would be the culprit that led to a very dark experience. Two years after high school, my best friend was killed in a hit-and-run accident in South Laguna Beach, California. I was able to diagnose myself with having clinical depression. I could not eat, drink, or sleep, yet alone smile and tap into my happiness gene.

During this time my mom was constantly trying to feed me applesauce. I have no clue why applesauce—she was like the dad in *My Big Fat Greek Wedding* who used Windex for everything. But nothing worked. She even went so far as to put affirmations everywhere, even on a mirror with lipstick. Nothing worked.

As time progressed, I started sleeping too much and eating too much. I became an overeater, weighing 195 pounds. I hid my food, empty wrappers, boxes, and dirty dishes like a drug addict hides their paraphernalia.

You know the saying "wherever you go there you are"? I enrolled in the University California San Diego, and I took all the pain with me. I fainted my first day of college and was in the infirmary all day. I was working full time, going to school, and trying to have a social life. Having absolutely no life skills training, trauma was catching up with me.

My subconscious mind probably was picking up on the clues. I decided to take an elective course titled "The Psychology of Suicide." What I am about to share with you was so life-altering. One day in class the parents of a young girl shared how their daughter committed suicide by jumping off the Coronado Bridge. She was a happy girl, or so everyone thought. Her picture showed her joy. I related to her. I too was living behind a happy face.

After that day, I knew I needed to make a decision: either to withdraw from the school or stay. My decision came on Christmas Eve 1993. I was sitting in my condo, curtains drawn, watching *Casablanca* with a glass of wine in my hand; it was noon. It was not the picture of a healthy young lady. Then the phone rang, and it was Nicole. She shared a quote with me: "Delete the need to understand everything. We don't need to understand *everything*; some things just are." Eventually I put the wine down, got dressed, and went home for the holidays. When I returned to school, I withdrew and enrolled in CSU San Marcos.

Then June 12, 1994, happened. I was awakened at 6:30 a.m. by horrific screams from Denise. It was like I had ever heard. Nicole was just thirty-five when she was murdered, and I was twenty-four. She left two children behind. The pain of losing her was not nearly as painful as watching my parents suffer. Overnight my family went from private to public. No one trains you on how to handle this. Multiple helicopters hovered over our home every single day for months; TV satellite trucks parked across the street, honing in on our every conversation. It was very intrusive. It is too surreal to put into words. Mom held my hand and said, "That is my kid" when we turned on the TV. I will never forget that moment.

Time goes on, and with that healing follows. I met a man who eventually would become my fiancé. We were planning to get married on September 11, 2004. And then he canceled the wedding—four days before! I went spinning into a dark tornado of pain, anger, fear, and hatred. I had never experienced emotions like these before. I went to a psychiatrist, and he prescribed Kolonopin, an antianxiety medication. I abused it and drank wine with it. I felt no pain—I was filing the "hole in my soul" with something self-destructive. Slowly my pain was seeping from my pores.

Then, on October 9, 2004, I snapped! I lashed out at everyone. I almost hit my dad, and I called my sister Denise horrible names. I proceeded to my bedroom where I saw my pills. I poured them into my left hand and grabbed a bottle of wine in the other. Just as I was about to pop them, Dominique stopped me. I still took four. I said, "Get me out of here before I hurt myself or someone else." The next day, I was in a psychiatric unit.

We all have experienced some sort of pain. Whether it's the loss of a loved one, a job, or a pet, when you don't have coping skills, how do you get through it? I learned the hard way, by being admitted to the hospital. I was never a patient or a victim. I was there, in the University of Life, as I like to call it. I knew I did not want to walk out the same person who came in. I learned tools to equip me for life. I am human and still crack at times. But eventually I get back on the train and dig in my toolbox. My biggest lesson, especially with recent events in my life, is to disengage. However, I still react at times. I am still a work in progress. We all are. Get real!

In the psychiatric unit, I was in a safe place where I could release everything. I learned coping skills to find peace amid my chaos. What was the outcome? I wrote my memoir, *Finding Peace amid the Chaos: My Escape from Depression and Suicide*, and I created The T.A.N.Y.A Formula, a five-step process for self-care and optimal mental and emotional WELL-BEing. I'm committed to sharing my story and strategies so what happened to me and my sister does not happen to you! My story of loss, grief, depression, and survival go beyond any monetary success I have attained. Today, I can honestly say that I am forever grateful for the trauma I have experienced because it has given me the gift of L.I.F.E. (Living Is For Everyone). I am able to give hope and healing to those who struggle with deep-seated issues or just everyday chaos. My job is to provide tools to fill their toolbox (self-care strategies) so they can manage their lives. I am passionate about this, because I really should not be here today.

Tanya Brown is no stranger to adversity or trauma. With the loss of her sister, Nicole Brown Simpson, she has faced overwhelming life challenges but has used these obstacles to ultimately improve the quality of her life. She is a domestic violence advocate, speaking and training people about the horror of abuse at home.

Ten years after the loss of Nicole, Tanya suffered a mental breakdown, and as a result, she is personally committed to speak on how to overcome adversity and promote healthy *mental health for overall well-being. She encourages her audiences to find peace amid daily chaos and learn the tools for integrating self-care for a life of optimal wellness.*

She is a nationally recognized author, speaker, and life coach who uses the lessons from her experience with Nicole and her own suicide attempt to help others cope with life's challenges. Her story makes it clear that you can overcome any adversity with the willingness to ask for help.

www.tanyabrown.net

THE POWER OF SPEAKING
"WITHOUT WALLS"

Lynn Rose

Deep in the pulsing underbelly of the Las Vegas Hilton Convention Center, eight thousand eager participants are filing into the main room to kick off their three-day event. They're bristling with excitement, as many of their famous favorites will be speaking to them throughout the three days.

Bob Eubanks was to be their emcee, and a number of stellar speakers adorn the featured list, including Jack Canfield, Mark Victor Hansen, John Gray, and John DeMartini (these luminaries also happen to be those sitting in the audience waiting for the festivities to begin).

Little do these eight thousand eager souls know that not only is Bob Eubanks *not* going to be their emcee as he had been every year, but their fearless leader and president of their company has done something unprecedented. He's taken Mr. Eubanks off the bill in order to put a complete unknown on in his stead.

Mr. President (we'll call him that for now) had seen her at a recent event, and though he had already had his event booked for months in advance, he shifted around his layout of the event so that this fresh face could kick off the entire thing. He decided to have this energizing lady start everyone off in song and then give them a motivating, uplifting, activating keynote—and then have her continue to act as an emcee for the remaining two days, sharing the responsibilities with Mr. Eubanks once the next day began.

WOW.

What an opportunity for this young lady! What an honor to be plucked from the virtual unknown and thrust into the forefront to share all her glory, talents, and gifts—in front of many of her heroes from the personal growth world who would be out there.

The stage is typical of these all-out corporate events. Video screens three stories tall act as the backdrop across what must be the size of a football field of a stage. A full orchestra is positioned stage left to play for her opening song and accompany the play-ons and play-offs for her and the other speakers.

What a perfect setting! What a perfect opportunity! Or is it? . . .

Ever notice how there are hidden worlds all around us? Things aren't exactly as they seem.

We have no idea of the hidden stories that lie beneath the surface of everyone we meet or every moment we encounter.

Such was the case with this "perfect" moment.

You see, this young lady had only ever spoken a few times before—she was green as green could be when it came to motivational speaking.

Sure, she'd sung, emceed, and hosted TV and radio for most of her adult life, but actual keynote speaking was a new and completely different animal for her.

Plus little did this huge audience know that she had flown in on a red-eye the night before, thus having *zero* sleep. Not only that, but upon arriving and meeting with the president and organizers to prep for the evening, they had promptly tossed out the speech she'd planned and totally rewrote it right there on the spot with her.

Yes, the *day of* the big night!

Oh, not to mention that there was *no* teleprompter anywhere on this big stage and *no* podium to keep some guideline notes or outline . . . you know . . . just in case . . .

Needless to say, as the hour was drawing closer, she may have made sure her hair, makeup, and dress were perfect, but as the welcoming music was crescendoing, as the lights were flashing throughout the audience to create a buzz and build anticipation, as the stagehands were bustling about with last minute preparations, this "unknown" was sitting on her stool, alone in her dressing room backstage, bent over in literal physical pain from the stress, debilitating fear, and overwhelming pressure.

Oh my God! I can't do this! I don't know what I'm doing, and I'm not ready! How the hell am I going to remember this speech? What if I forget the words? What if these folks don't like me—they don't even know me! Oh my God, all these leaders in personal growth that I've admired and looked up to all my life will see me utterly fail right in front of them . . . oh dear Lord, I'm going to disappoint this poor president who's taken a huge risk with me . . . I can't even stand up, I'm so sick! What do I do? Oh God, please! I'll do anything! Just make the fire alarms go off so that they have to kick everyone out of the convention hall and the night gets cancelled . . .help meeeeee! These thoughts swirled all around and through her unendingly.

The worst part was that it had triggered that old distant familiar feeling she had had for a certain period of time in her life. Oh my goodness, there it was again, taking over her body yet again after all these years. Pure, un-adulterated fear and utter shut-down mode.

It hearkened back to a particular time from her past, a time where, after appearing on Broadway and TV and other successes, trauma from her past came back to haunt her and she became completely unable to perform at all.

She could barely speak, barely get any sound out, and any attempt to perform was worse than the most rank amateur—almost like a bad *Saturday Night Live* skit. The mere thought of it was painful, no less the memory of how deeply embarrassing and horrendous the experience had been back then.

Thankfully, after two years of cocooning in order to heal, and having to leave the entertainment industry to survive, she was able to find her way back, stronger than ever and had had a robust career from that time forward.

However, here were echoes of that long-ago time, threatening to take over, along with every other possible "demon" one could imagine.

So how the heck did this gal get through this? *Did* she fail miserably? Was her career over before it even began?

How can *anyone* perform under that type of pressure, in the midst of experiencing that level of all-consuming doubt, limiting beliefs, fears, pressure, and exhaustion?

Well, we'll get to that in a moment, but first, let me share with you, "that girl," if you haven't guessed it by now, was *me*.

And I had a definitive moment in the midst of that obliterating swirl.

I knew I had to call on everything I had within me, everything I'd ever learned in the world of performing, and everything I knew within.

Don't get me wrong; it's not about "just click your heels three times and you're good to go."

No, it takes focus, it takes determination, it takes courage, and it takes being willing to take on *all* of who you are and walk through that muck in order to take on the *full* power of what you have to share, and give it all you've got when you hit the stage, stepping in front of a camera, or even just presenting in front of clients.

It takes the commitment to not let yourself decide that "you can't do it" or that "you don't have what it takes" or that "you'll fail if you try."

No matter where you are in your own process, no matter how you feel, no matter how much experience you may have had (or not had), and no matter what your circumstances, the *good* news is that it's possible to navigate through anything you face.

This is the power of what I call "speaking without walls." And this is what I called upon to turn what seemed like a hopeless, doomed situation into what became a triumphant launching and now a successful international speaking career.

With trembling knees, I took on this very type of approach, thinking, technique, and being-ness that I train all those who go through my WOW process to be able to do, and, like a warrior sailing with the wind at her back, I was able to dance my way through terror and excitement, jitters and joy, and shift from shutdown to sheer success.

I almost collapsed when I came off that stage. The blur of congratulatory praise and celebration was like looking through a foggy window, but one thing remains clear: when you "speak without walls," when you own who you are, when you are willing to truly connect to an audience and trust to be led from that connection, *that's* when your real brilliance can come through.

The wonderful irony is that to this day, I still use a brief video clip from that event for some of my promotional materials.

And to this day, I share this message and lead trainings on how to instill, at a cellular level, this whole other way of coming at speaking—one that dissolves everything you've ever thought speaking was "supposed" to be.

So many approaches to speaking or presentations address it from an external perspective. There's nothing wrong with that, and it has served millions of people. But that particular way ends up taking a long time for someone to master it to the point where they *own* it and it flows effortlessly and naturally. And they *still* may find themselves having no idea what to do if they're suddenly thrown into a situation where there is no preparation or circumstances aren't the most ideal.

The WOW approach that I've created, cultivated, and crafted gives that ability to you within minutes once you know what to do. It's truly amazing to know that you have the ability to *shine* no matter what. You *can* WOW your audiences, your clients, your videos every time, no matter what.

Perhaps someday I may have the honor of personally connecting with you and seeing you reveal your brilliance to its fullest. Or perhaps you'll at least remember to let who you are come out to play, trust being led from your connection, and let the magic of YOU happen.

Whatever path you choose, dare to live and speak without walls.

Lynn Rose is a highly sought-after International keynoter, emcee, and entertainer for Fortune 500 events. She's a celebrated media entrepreneur, performance and leadership expert and the CEO of The Power To WOW. She has spoken or performed for millions of people at thousands of events around the world, while helping others make their own successful global impact as well.

Seen on: CBS, ABC, NBC, Sony, and other TV, film, and media, Lynn has shared the stage with Mariah Carey, Jay Leno, Stevie Wonder, Meryl Streep, Tony Robbins, Deepak Chopra, and more.

Behind the scenes, she's known as "The WOWMaker," as for over a decade, she has worked with billion-dollar CEOs, celebrities, and thought leaders, helping them bring out their "WOW" when they speak, pitch, or perform.

Her clients have gone on to host major network TV shows, become well-known thought leaders and business celebrities, New York Times *Bestselling authors, and rise to fame as the go-to leader in their specific industry, some bringing in seven- and eight-figure incomes as a result.*

www.LynnRose.com
Lynn@LynnRose.com

GROWING UP TO BE A ROCK STAR

Nancy Matthews

I think I've always wanted to be a Rock Star. As far back as I can remember, rock 'n' roll has been a driving force for my optimism, my hopes, and my desire to be a Rock Star!

As a little girl growing up in Brooklyn, New York, my friends and I would hold concerts in the backyard, playing our 45s (for those who don't remember, they are small records with a big hole with only one song on each side), and singing our hearts out to the cheering audience of our supportive parents. The stage continued to call me, and I joined the chorus, got parts in school plays, and even learned how to play guitar.

But then something happened, and I stopped it all.

- Was it because I switched schools in tenth grade and felt out of place in my new school?
- Was it because I was overweight and ridiculed by my classmates, causing me to become self-conscious and afraid to get out on stage?
- Was it because, when I was fifteen, my father died from alcoholism?
- Was it because I had started smoking pot (and lots of it), and my desire and motivation got blurred through the haze?

I'm not sure which of these, or perhaps some other still undiscovered occurrence, caused me to stop pursuing my dream of being a Rock Star, but while that dream got temporarily halted, rock 'n' roll never stopped filling my soul.

My record collection began to grow. I went to every live show I could and was continuously inspired by the music, the lyrics, and the entrepreneurial spirit of the Rock Stars who had gone for their dreams in big ways. It was during this time that one particular performer seemed to get so deep inside my soul that I began to dream again and believe I could do it too!

That performer, entertainer, entrepreneur, author, speaker, and icon is the one, the only . . . Bruce Springsteen. In fact, I've gone to close to one hundred of his shows, and one of my favorite spots to be is behind the stage. From this vantage point I get to feel what it's like to move thousands of people—to have them sing your lyrics and raise their hands—and take them on three-hour journey that has them leave feeling fulfilled, inspired, and connected to each other through the bond of your message.

As I look back on my early seeds of desire to be a Rock Star, that is what fueled me . . . how the audience responded, reacted, and was moved by what was shared on stage. And it is that same desire to make a positive impact in peoples' lives that has brought me back to the stage, singing my song!

I now have the privilege of inspiring and entertaining audiences to lift them up to go for their big dreams and provide the tools and resources for them to achieve them. Whether I'm in a one-on-one conversation, speaking to audiences, or meeting people on the street, the fuel still comes from the same place: to make a positive impact in the life of every person I meet.

That desire resulted in my book The One Philosophy, which shares simple principles for living the way of "The One."

- The One who truly cares about every person they meet because "Everyone's The One."
- The One who is fully present in every conversation, honoring that particular moment in time.
- The One who takes the time to reflect and go within to fulfill their heart's desires and vision to bring their unique contribution to the world.

The journey from the fifteen-year-old girl who put down her guitar and silenced her voice to the woman who is now an international speaker, best-selling author, and yes . . . Rock Star with her very own song has been a journey filled with highs and lows, twists and turns, and of course, ups and downs. It is most likely similar to the journey you've been on in this grand roller coaster of life.

While I know that every step of my journey was meant to be and that looking back with regret would only limit where I still want to go, there are a few lessons I wish I had learned earlier. I share some of those with you here as you reach higher and higher to experience life and fulfill your highest potential as the Rock Star you were born to be.

R Remember you were born to be extraordinary. Don't let others' opinions of you stop you from taking action and pursuing what matters to you.

O Obstacles are only meant to build your persistence and innovation muscles, not stop you.

C Change is natural. Learn to go with the flow of the tides and "oh, the places you'll go!"

K Keep your chin up even in down times. Lifting your chin triggers hormones that inspire creative thinking, and that's where the solutions to your troubled times will come about.

O Open up to receive support from others. You're not meant to fulfill your vision alone.

N Notice the signs. Seeds of desire sprout into buds of opportunity. Stay alert and aware to see the opportunities and take inspired action.

May the music within always remind you that you live in the promised land of hope and dreams and that you're "The One!"

Be The One who makes a positive difference in the world around you. Be The One who goes for their goals and dreams with gusto and love. Be The One who treats every person as "The One" . . . because "Everyone's The One."

Go to TheOnePhilosophy.com/song for a free download of the song and an invitation to join in the mission of feeding peoples' bodies and souls by living the way of The One.

Nancy Matthews brings more than thirty years of experience and the perfect blend of business expertise, authenticity, and heart to all of her endeavors. After twenty years in corporate with several entrepreneurial endeavors on the side, in 2002 Nancy went into business for herself, eventually developing several multimillion dollar enterprises. As a single mother of two amazing children, she knows first-hand how to juggle the many demands on a woman's time and energy to achieve extraordinary goals and enjoy the journey! She is the founder of Women's Prosperity Network, a global organization serving women in business.

Author of The One Philosophy, Visionaries with Guts, *the highly acclaimed* Receiving Your Riches *course, and the bestselling series* Journey to the Stage, *Nancy is regularly featured in the media and has shared the stage with some of today's top thought leaders and business experts.*

NancyMatthews.com
WomensProsperityNetwork.com

SHADY SKYES

Lisa Reed

I got married on a whim. A drunken Fourth of July in 1990 turned into a trip to Vegas for an early morning wedding. Dressed in a black mini-dress and sandals, with him in jeans and a Cinco-de-Mayo T-shirt, we said our "I dos" and bought a ring at the local pawnshop. My groom had just joined the rock band, Guns N' Roses, entertaining millions and touring the world. Along with the glitz and glamour that went along with touring came the chaos of rock-n-roll. GNR were notorious for their unpredictable concerts and fans who would passionately display their emotions in the oddest and most extreme ways. We toured for most of the first year of our marriage, and when we came home in 1991, I was pregnant. At the time, we were living in North Hollywood, and in June of 1992, when Skye entered this world, in a swirl of earthquakes and aftershocks, I expressed to Dizzy that NOHO was not where I planned on raising our children. I grew up in the pristine beach town of Dana Point, so I suggested that we transplant our new family there to be closer to my parents, who could help me with the baby while he was on tour. Dizzy agreed, and we moved the two hours south.

The next year we continued touring, bringing Skye with us. As mentioned, GNR fans can be intense, and traveling with an infant was pretty terrifying at times. In Italy a fan ripped Skye's stuffed Snoopy—whom she had named "Uhoh"—out of her little hands as we were leaving the hotel, attempting to steal it. Thanks to a quick knock to the fan's head and fast hands by security, Uhoh was retrieved and we were carried the rest of the way to the van. (Thanks, Truck!) Another time, fans approached us in Barcelona knowing every detail of Skye's birth, and this was before the Internet. It was unnerving, to say the least.

Between the craziness of the road, the aggressive fans, and the riots or near riots that seemed to plague GNR, raising kids in this kind of chaos was challenging. I totally understand people wanting to lock themselves behind iron gates, with 24/7 security, but I was adamant that I would not raise spoiled "rockstar" kids. Dizzy and I had both been fortunate enough to have idyllic childhoods in suburbia, and we wanted the same for our children.

When the tour ended, GNR was recording in LA. The commute was three hours each way up the 405, and it was slowly killing Dizzy. Much to my chagrin, we decided we needed to move closer to the city. I was determined to give my kids the suburban life. I wanted them to ride their bikes in cul-de-sacs and go to public schools. We agreed on a town thirty miles north of Los Angeles called Thousand Oaks. In my opinion, it was too far from the ocean, but it was the perfect place to raise a family. I couldn't walk to the beach, but I could drive there in twenty minutes, and Dizzy could be at the studio in thirty. A new compromise was made.

Two years later Shade was born. We had a new house built in a quaint community called Wood Ranch. Life was ideal. The girls rode bikes in the cul-de-sac, rode horses in the hills, and excelled in martial arts, and I worked with emotionally disturbed teens.

GNR had gone through a lot of changes, but they were touring and fans loved it. The days of insanity were gone. Juicers had replaced whiskey backstage, and children replaced groupies for the most part. I'm sure the rock 'n' roll stereotypes still occurred when the wives weren't around, but that's the life.

In 2002 that life came crashing down. Due to circumstances that I am not 100 percent sure of, riots occurred in Canada and Philadelphia. The promoter panicked, canceled the tour, and sent everyone home. The proverbial shit hit the fan. Our income was frozen due to lawsuits from every which way. My salary didn't cover our bills, and a huge new whirlwind of chaos hit our family. Dizzy and I buckled down to do what we needed to do get our family through this challenge. We sold our house and relocated to a smaller home. I got a second job while Dizzy picked up gigs in Hollywood, and we survived day to day.

I was always the optimist in our marriage, but during the years between 2002 and 2009, that optimism faded. I was tired of working two jobs. The upheaval of our lives caused our marriage to suffer, but I tried to keep life as normal as possible. We attempted to hide our problems, and I thought we were doing just that, until at one of Axl's parties, he called me out. He told Beta, his assistant and right-hand goddess, that I was too skinny and asked her to find out what was wrong with me. He was the only person I hadn't fooled.

Despite the discord in our marriage, we were a united front when it came to parenting. Dizzy became the awesome PTA dad, while I worked to make sure we survived. We reached another compromise. But sometimes, no matter how much you compromise, it just isn't enough.

In 2009 it all crumbled. Choices were made, making it impossible for our marriage to continue. We parted as friends and divorced in 2010. The kids—especially Shade—took it the hardest, but I kept their lives as normal as possible. School issues and mental health issues plagued us. Skye was working her hardest in community college, and Shade struggled through high school. It was hard work just to keep them healthy and sane. This was the roughest part of my life, but we made it through together.

In 2013 Skye was accepted to the University of Oklahoma, and moved to Norman, where she met and married Robert. She graduated with a bachelor's degree in biology and applied to vet schools. She was rejected twice, but she persisted and was accepted to Ross University of Veterinary Medicine in St. Kitts. This amazing woman moved to a Caribbean island, 2,500 miles away from her new husband and family, and still finished her first semester with a 4.0.

Shade graduated from high school at the age of sixteen, after years of fighting the system. Her logic was that if she could ace the tests, why do the homework? I agreed with her, but I told her she needed to learn to play the game. She's still learning that, but she has become a strong, independent woman, and is currently working on an album with her dad. I know she will reach her own dreams despite the adversity of her past. She is just as determined and talented as her sister.

We have all made it through the combined chaos of rock 'n' roll, divorce, and mental health issues. If we hadn't gone through the financial calamity and its adverse effects, I sometimes wonder if my girls would have developed the same tenacity and independence. I believe that the hardships have made them stronger. They know the meaning of a dollar, hard work, and determination through chaos. So many of their peers became statistics with drugs, teenage pregnancies, and drunk driving. Society would have believed that our kids would have been prime examples of these statistics, because they are "rockstar" offspring, but they weren't! They excelled and broke the stereotype! I attribute this to perseverance, positivity, and love. To me, this is the ultimate success.

My independent, strong children have morphed into women whose futures are destined to be bigger and brighter than ever. These children make me proud, and I am so lucky to be their mother. My optimistic views on life have returned thanks to them, and I once again feel like a rockstar when I think of all of their accomplishments. I know 99 percent of the credit goes to them, but I would like to think that 1 percent is due to my own tenacity and determination. I hope they learned these qualities from me, at least a little bit. These children are my greatest success, and I thank the stars for them every minute of every day.

Lisa Reed is by vocation a sensational writer and by profession a retired special education paraprofessional. Through her twenty-year marriage to Dizzy Reed of Guns N' Roses, she was right at the center of rock 'n' roll. A born-and-raised Californian, Lisa now resides in Oklahoma with her daughter Shade and a menagerie of dogs. Lisa is currently working on her memoirs about her life, as a wife, and raising a family in the insanity of the rock 'n' roll world.

MUSIC: THE RECIPE FOR LOVE

Tesy Ward

The recipe for financial success is the same as it has always been: work hard and never give up. However, success itself can be measured in many ways. What I have always considered more important than any financial success I have achieved, is the time I devote to giving back to those who may not have been granted some of the same opportunities I was blessed to have access to.

Success can be as simple as the rewarding feeling of helping someone else achieve something, whether it's a simple goal or a lifelong dream. We all need to exercise our spiritual muscles in order to reach our peak and carry others along as we journey through life. It is for this reason that I enjoy representing artists as much as I enjoy being one. I strongly believe music is food for the soul. However, it is the first program to disappear in schools when budgets become constrained. Nothing breaks my heart more. Many years ago, I started devoting my time and personal resources toward developing programs to ensure that music—both the listening to and expression of—was not lost to those most at risk to poverty and peril within our marginalized communities.

What I firmly believe is that most troubled souls, particularly those of our youth, our future, crave an opportunity to see that there is palpable hope, to believe that someone truly cares about them. In other words, they need to know that love is not lost; they have not been abandoned.

Seeing a group of beautiful children open up to music has been more rewarding than words can express. The simple act of sharing music, along with some nutritious food and clean water, is all that is necessary to restore a forgotten smile, a twinkle of happiness to their eyes, a joyful bounce to their step. Shadows of darkness and defeat quickly give way to the light of love, to rays of hope, and to endless potential. What's miraculous about the redemptive qualities of music is that you do not need to be a skilled musician, nor an accomplished vocalist. Two ears—or lacking those, the sense of touch—is all that is necessary to activate the gateways music uses to permeate the soul in a deep and meaningful way.

The expression "music is the universal language" is a phrase often tossed about. Its overuse has severely diluted its message. It comes full strength once again when the inspiring force that is music ignites the soul of the forlorn and prompts them to choose victory over defeat, legal over illegal, hope over despair. A tattered, oppressed child is instantly restored, with a full accompaniment of life choices and dreams to be attained. This effect lasts, not for as long as the beat plays through the sound system, but far more deeply and permanently within the recesses of the listeners' souls. It is truly life-changing to witness.

I shared these dreams of bringing music to children and the oppressed with my beloved friend, Andy Gibb, who would have turned sixty on March 5, 2018. Sadly, he was lost to all who love him on March 10, 1988. I will be forever indebted to Andy, his brother Barry, and his beloved nephew, Stephen, for all their contributions to my life and my musical endeavors. Andy was a deeply caring and compassionate man whose heart overflowed with love for children, family, and music. I celebrate and honor his memory within the sentiments expressed in this book. I encourage everyone to follow in Andy's footsteps and share your gifts, and most importantly your love.

Tesy Ward is a successful businesswoman, philanthropist, and multiple bestselling author, known for her ability to identify, cultivate, and bring to market "hidden gems" within the music and entertainment industries. Her unique approach to business emanates from a lifetime of experience as a singer, lyricist, and developer of musical talent.

www.TesyWard.com

FROM SURVIVING HOLLYWOOD
TO COMMANDING MY OWN STAGE

Melody Keymer Harper

Whatever interest group or age group I speak to, I hear one question asked most often: "How and why did you become a professional speaker?" Here is how it all came about.

At the age of three, my mom entered my twin sister and me in a talent contest at a local market in San Gabriel, California, where I grew up. Wearing knee-length green dresses with white collars and puffy short sleeves, white ankle socks with lace, and shiny little black Mary Jane shoes, we looked like two little "Shirley Temples" with curly brown hair. We sang in unison to the tune of "I Love You a Bushel and a Peck," the song our mom used to sing to us after reading each night before going to sleep.

I was hooked! The minute the audience roared and cheered in response to our performance, I instantly fell in love with singing on stage. Winning first place, we received a huge bag of groceries for our family. For a young child, that was quite a reward for doing something so fun. This was my first learning experience of using eye contact with an audience, projecting my voice, and smiling.

By the time I was ten, I was getting paid to sing in productions on radio and TV variety shows, while being raised like the girl next door. I did not attend Hollywood High or get homeschooled like other child actors I knew. Instead, I attended my local public schools and participated in all the school clubs and activities.

At the age of sixteen, my sister and I landed the twin lead roles of Jan and Jill in a TV series pilot called *The Jackson Twins*, costarring actors Dennis O'Keefe and Jan Clayton playing our parents. Not only did we act our parts, we sang the show's theme song. The pilot got picked up quickly and was scheduled to air.

As fortune would have it, Patty Duke had just won the Best Actress Oscar for her role as Helen Keller in the movie *The Miracle Worker*. Unlike today, where there are numerous shows of the same genre being aired, at that time there was only one detective story, one medical program, one sitcom, and so forth. After receiving her Oscar, sponsors raced into production for *The Patty Duke Show*, where she played both parts of look-alike cousins. Needless to say, the Best Actress Oscar trumped singing identical twins. Patty's show got aired, and ours got shelved! I learned that disappointments will happen in life and it is important to keep focused on your goals.

Mom entered my twin and me as a single entry in the Miss Los Angeles Beauty Pageant when we were seventeen. Everything we did had to be perfectly synchronized. We won the title and went on to win first runner-up to Miss California in the Miss America Pageant. This taught me the power of organization, stage presence, attention to details, and teamwork.

Performing as the Gemini Twins in the live stage play *A Funny Thing Happened on the Way to the Forum*, starring Mickey Rooney and Jose Ferrer, offered me a great learning experience in professionalism, being in the moment, and involving the audience in a performance.

Then it happened! During my television interview with Johnny Carson on *The Tonight Show*, I experienced my first real bout of stage fright—in front of hundreds of people in his audience and millions watching on their home TVs. I froze! My hands were shaking, I broke out in a sweat, and my mind went totally blank. I couldn't speak! Afterward Johnny shared with me how he handled his own stage fright, which I now share with my clients.

When I acted with Elvis Presley in the movie *Double Trouble*, I asked Elvis if he ever had stage fright. He shared, "Every time I get on stage, I get them butterflies in my stomach, but them butterflies is what keeps me at the top of my performance." Like Johnny, Elvis offered strategies he used to control his nervousness.

By nineteen I had achieved membership with three theatrical unions: American Federation of Television and Radio Artists (AFTRA), American Equity Association (AEA) for performing on live stage, and the Screen Actors Guild (SAG) for acting in film.

Observing how conscientiously my sister and I were raised, agents, producers, and directors were very protective of us on the sets and kept us under their wings. One producer told us that "the walls have ears" and you never know who is listening. Many a child prodigy was blackballed due to inappropriate behavior and attitudes. Another producer escorted us back to our personal trailer after each scene so we wouldn't mingle with any "bad" influence. Elvis invited us to join him with his "boy entourage" at his house for a party. The director strongly cautioned us not to go to any of Elvis' wild and out of control parties. I learned to wisely select what I say, present myself in the best light, and carefully weigh my decisions.

While continuing to work in show biz, I attended college and earned both bachelor and master's degrees along with two teaching and school counseling credentials. Merging my show biz experience with teaching, counseling, and consulting has given me the opportunity to present hundreds of keynote speeches, seminars, and workshops for thousands of people, helping them overcome barriers, deliver compelling messages, and build their businesses.

In my Ignite Your Speaking Power three-day events and consulting programs, I share show biz, educational, and life stories I've learned over the years regarding how to manage stage fright, be authentic, communicate with confidence, and monetize your message. To this day I still get so much fulfillment and joy from helping my clients transform their businesses from being mediocre to highly successful in their industry through mastering the art of public speaking and communication.

Melody Keymer Harper is a highly sought-after speaker, bestselling author, and consultant with thirty-plus years of experience teaching successful speaking and communication strategies to Create Unstoppable Confidence, Make an Impact, and Grow Your Business Through Mastering the Art of Public Speaking and Communication.

Aside from acting in the movie Double Trouble *with Elvis Presley, Melody has also shared the stage and screen with speaking giants such as Brian Tracy, Les Brown, and Jack Canfield and celebrities such as Johnny Carson, Betty White, Elizabeth Taylor, Mickey Rooney, Debbie Reynolds, Ricky Nelson, and Helen Reddy.*

Melody's personalized consulting programs transform people from mediocre to highly successful public speakers and communicators in their industry.

www.IgniteYourSpeakingPower.com

HOW TO GET UN-STUCK IN 30 DAYS

Linda Kruse

Recently, one of my best friends of thirty years suddenly passed away, and it hit me like a ton of bricks. I felt that her life had been "half-lived," and that awful feeling made me contemplate my own mortality. Unable to eat, sleep, work or work out, I was seriously stuck. After collecting a lot of advice, I realized that feeling hopelessly "stuck" at some point in our lives is a common experience. This prompted me to create **30 Ways to Get Un-stuck in 30 Days.** If you feel "stuck," I encourage you to implement and/or repeat at least one, if not a handful of these, each day.

1. Mark Your Calendar: Thirty days from today: Give yourself permission to have that day be the day you will start feeling better. Save that date. Work toward that day.

2. Play Soft Sounds: Put on instrumental music and/or the gentle babbling sound of water in the background. Nothing distracting—just whatever is soothing to you.

3. Organize: Clean out a place that's been bugging you—a linen closet, the medicine cabinet—any place that requires no deep thought. Grab the junk drawer or a stack of magazines, a trash can, and watch TV while you sort, clean, and toss the clutter.

4. Dance: Crank up that music from your high school days, and sing and dance like no one is watching.

5. Read: Revisit your favorite motivational book with new eyes, or go to a bookstore and see what moves you. Try: *Pivot: The Only Move That Matters Is Your Next One* by Jenny Blake.

6. Escape: Go out to the movies alone or binge-watch your favorite old films at home.

7. Bake: Measuring and creating helps get you out of your head. Make individual portions and give them away to the mailman or neighbors. Freeze treats for the next time someone pops by unexpectedly.

8. Exercise: Lay out your gym clothes each night so the first thing you do is put them on. And don't negotiate by saying: "I'll workout Monday, Wednesday and Friday." When Monday comes, don't stay in bed and negotiate again: "I'll workout extra hard tomorrow, Thursday, and Saturday." Tuesday will come and you'll still be negotiating. Do something every day, and you won't negotiate with yourself.

9. Eat Healthier: Food affects your mood. Be aware of what you eat. Make small changes: eat fresh; limit processed food and caffeine; avoid sugar. Use an app to track your progress and make healthier choices.

10. Garden: Put your hands in the dirt and focus on nurturing something to life. Try plants that produce quickly: beets, broccoli, cucumbers, green onions, kale, and lettuce—all grow within two months. Plant and watch them grow.

11. Call a Friend: Try to speak less and listen more. Really listen.

12. Pray: Find your God, your Angel, your way of praying; open your mind to receive guidance.

13. Indulge in Alone Time: Go to the beach or climb a hill. Clear your head and see if you can discover what's next.

14. Fix Your Home: Make a list, room by room, of every little thing that needs fixing. In the margins write the length of time it will take to complete each task. Then, whenever you have twenty minutes, check that list for a twenty-minute task. You'll be surprised how easy it is to find time to fix the things that can be fixed.

15. Volunteer: Feed the homeless. Build homes with Habitat for Humanity. Find a charity to support. The GuideStar directory has over

1.8 million nonprofit charities and organizations: https://www.guidestar.org/NonprofitDirectory.aspx.

16. Go to Church: Better yet, visit the services of a different faith and learn from the perspective of "we grow more together."

17. Watch Ted Talks: There are over 2,600 "talks" to stir your curiosity: https://www.ted.com/talks.

18. Use "Yes and . . .": In improv there is an exercise called "Yes, and . . ." that allows the action to always move forward. What would happen if you responded with "Yes, and . . ." to your daily life? Try it for a day. Say "yes and . . ." to everything.

19. Play with Animals: Visit a local dog park, an animal rescue, or a nature sanctuary. You'll find more at: http://www.humanedecisions.com/list-of-animal-sanctuaries-in-the-u-s/.

20. Spend Time with an Older Person: Andy Rooney once said, "The best classroom in the world is at the feet of an elderly person." Older people are full of wisdom . . . and riddles that take a lifetime to figure out. Things like: "Be careful how you waste your time," and "There are always sign-posts along the way." But the insights they share are priceless.

21. Practice Yoga: The very heart of yoga is abyhasa—"steady effort in the direction you want to go." There is always room for change, but you must be open to it.

22. Avoid Negative Self-Talk: We all "speak" to ourselves, even when it's not out loud (i.e., "You're such an idiot"). How we treat ourselves reflects what we think of ourselves. Listen to what you say to yourself and, if it's negative, adjust it. Try Power Thought Cards by Louise L. Hay: "Every thought I think is a creation of my future."

23. Remove Negative Thoughts: The most powerful form of positive thinking happens when you don't allow doubt to creep into your thoughts. Whenever a negative thought knocks, deny it entry. Chase it away. Discredit it. Try it for a day and do it consistently; it will become easier, and you will manifest what you want.

24. Complete the CLEAN SWEEP Checklist: 100 items analyzing four areas: Physical Environment, Well-Being, Money, and Relationships – cornerstones for a strong and healthy life. Visit http://betterme.org/cleansweep.html.

25. Order the SELF Journal: a simple daily productivity planner that helps structure your day to reach goals sooner than you thought possible. Visit https://bestself.co/.

26. Set Very Specific Goals: Be as specific as possible. Give yourself a clear understanding of what successfully reaching your goal looks like: "Lose five pounds" is a better goal than "lose some weight." Think of specific actions: Promising yourself that you'll "sleep more" is too vague; be clear and precise. "I'll be in bed by 10 p.m. on weeknights" leaves no room for doubt. Knowing exactly what you intend to achieve will keep you motivated until you get there.

27. Pamper Yourself: Take a long bath. Get a massage or a mani-pedi once a month. Check Groupon and try a new place.

28. Plan an Event: A vacation, girls' weekend glamping trip, sbling trip, even a dinner party or meeting friends at a restaurant you haven't tried.

29. Re-Evaluate the People in Your Life: Avoid negative people. The people around you reinforce your thoughts. Spend more time with the ones that lift your spirit and empower you. You are the company you keep.

30. Practice the Art of Gratitude: Say "thank you" as often as possible. Instead of e-mailing or texting, write handwritten thank-you notes and actually mail them.

Graduation Day: This is the day you picked thirty days ago. You've developed a Practice of Self-Care: True self-care has very little to do with "treating yourself" and a whole lot do with making choices for your long-term wellness. You're living in a way that other people won't, so you can live in a way that other people can't. You're creating ways to enjoy life—not escape from it!

This chapter is dedicated to my amazingly talented and great friend, Monette Holderer Melvin: You lived in a way that others couldn't. I'll always miss you, Mo!

Linda Kruse is a news correspondent, international spokesperson, corporate trainer and documentarian. As a multi-award winning director, Linda's last documentary, KRUSING AMERICA, *won sixty awards, earning her both Filmmaker of the Year and Director of the Year. A best-selling author and an accomplished writer, Linda is currently featured in both number-one bestsellers:* Women Who Rock *and* Rock Your Life. *The owner of Atticus Productions, Inc., Linda has written, produced, and directed projects worldwide that explore challenging and intriguing topics while definitively capturing real people and the worlds they live in. All of her work is presented with a creative elegance that is her signature style. "How to Get Un-Stuck in 30 Days" is based on Linda's new online storytelling training series used to improve performance and inspire change.*

www.lindakruse.com

JOURNEY TO HEALTH

Gale Barbe

Why can't I remember the details? It happened so quickly.

I woke up one morning with a pain in my chest. I had a hard time breathing, and I knew something was wrong. I called my husband at work. He came home and took me to the emergency room.

After several tests, the result was that I had a pulmonary embolism. First all kinds of questions came flooding into my head. What is that? What does that mean? Why did this happen? What now? Then I started blaming myself and feeling guilty.

I should have taken better care of myself; I should have been eating healthier and working on losing all the weight I had put on through the years. I should have been exercising instead of leading a sedentary lifestyle. I had gotten so lazy, and I didn't have the energy to do anything about it. Not only was I in terrible physical health, but my emotional health was just as bad, if not worse. I knew I had to do something or I'd be dead at a very young age.

I had already lost my father, age sixty-three, and brother, age forty-three, due to unhealthy choices. I kept hoping, wishing, and wanting to be healthier, but I didn't have the motivation. I needed help! I then realized that my motivation was my daughter, Meagan, and my husband, Paul. I had to stop being so selfish and think about how life would be for them without me in it. That was more unbearable than the thought of me giving up on life and just dying. But life had become too difficult. I was in so deep that I couldn't pull myself out of the mess I was in.

Somehow hope kept me alive. I was hanging on to it for dear life. Thankfully I was too stubborn to give up. What was it going to take to turn my life around and make the changes I needed to make? My life had to be worth something other than just existing day in and day out. My doctor had been monitoring my health, had me on medications, and talked to me over and over about how I needed to lose weight. The hope that I was hanging on to led me to make a very tough but potentially lifesaving decision.

I had tried all kinds of diets, but none of them worked. Finally my doctor said to me, "Please reconsider doing gastric bypass surgery because all I'm doing is putting Band-Aids on you. Until you take the weight off, you will continue to have more problems physically and emotionally and take more and more medications." It was then that I totally accepted my need for help—I couldn't do it on my own.

I made the decision to go through the process to qualify and prepare for gastric bypass surgery. And what a process it was! My insurance company required that I take a six-month nutritional course and undergo psychiatric evaluation along with several other tests. For two weeks before the surgery I was required to be on a liquid protein diet. If I cheated and ate anything during those two weeks, the doctor would not do the surgery. This was required to reduce the fat around the liver in order for the doctor to access my stomach during surgery. This doctor does monthly informational seminars about the different weight loss surgeries and I was actually able to watch a video of the surgery!

None of this prepared me for what I was about to go through, however. I was nervous, scared, and skeptical. The most important thing I needed was the support of my family and the belief that it would all be OK. My faith was weak, and I had to rely on my family to give me a lot of encouragement.

The doctor doing the surgery has support groups in place that meet twice a month to help his patients with the journey they are going through. The dietitian and psychologist associated with the doctor's office answer questions and give guidance to patients. Going to these meetings was extremely helpful and allowed me to be vulnerable about my feelings. Hearing the experiences of other people who have been through the same thing was also reassuring. I learned that the people who follow the program and go to the meetings are the most successful.

After my surgery, the first six months were the most rewarding, as that is when I lost most of my weight. I was like a baby learning how to eat food. My new tiny stomach could not hold too much. I learned to be very mindful of what and how fast I was eating, ultimately paying attention to my stomach being full, but not too full. These six months are what they call the honeymoon phase. It gave me time to practice changes in my eating habits, and it gave me a big jump-start on my weight loss. After that it got more difficult to stay on track. Old habits started sneaking in, temptations got the best of me, and the weight started coming off slower.

I have lost over one hundred pounds, joined a fitness center, and continue to work toward losing more weight and getting healthier. Circumstances in life have thrown wrenches in my journey, and it's how I've dealt with them that affects my health every day.

This journey has by no means been easy! As with any journey, there are struggles and victories. I have learned many tools and techniques in the past few years that have helped me. It is through hope and faith that I keep moving forward and taking positive actions toward improving my health.

"He who has health, has hope;
and he who has hope, has everything."
—Thomas Carlyle

Gale Barbe is a dedicated mother and housewife. Since her daughter graduated from high school, she has struggled as an empty nester and has been on a journey to improve her physical and emotional health. Part of that journey has been getting certified as a master practitioner of NLP (Neuro Linguistic Programming), hypnotherapy, time techniques, EFT (Emotional Freedom Techniques), and success coaching. She is passionate about helping others with their health and happiness by using these tools and other natural and holistic practices.

www.galebarbe.com

FROM BACKHOE TO TECH CEO

Michelle Calloway

When I was eleven years old, my parents sent my brother and me away for the summer to work on their friend's ranch. My job as the only girl was to shadow the lady of the house and help her with cooking, cleaning, and tending to some of the farm animals.

I didn't really want to go, but my parents said it would be a good experience for me. At first I was intimidated by the woman I was assigned to work with. She was gruff and direct, and she seemed to enjoy bossing me around. I was far from home, and I wasn't used to someone other than my parents correcting me, and I didn't take it too well. I wanted to go home. I talked to the ranch owner, who was a kind man, and pleaded with him to take me home. He comforted me and said he agreed that the lady of the house could be difficult to work with, but that I should give it a little more time. He said once I got to know her, I'd see how special she really was. I felt a little better after that talk, so I agreed to give it one more week.

Things got better after that. He must have said something to her, because she stopped being so gruff when she had to correct me on how to do things. She quickly noticed that I wasn't very content being indoors all day. The boys got to be outside doing adventurous things like chopping wood, stacking hay, and tending to the barns. She began incentivizing me to reach goals so I could go outside and participate with the boys. I would whip through my chores so I could go outside, but she would only allow me to go out if she approved my work. I quickly learned that it didn't pay to be fast if your quality of work suffered. If I planned my day right and took fewer steps (as long as those steps were done well), I could reach my goal faster and get more time outside. Major WIN!

The more I took the incentive to produce quality work in an efficient manner, the more privileges I began to receive. I respected those privileges and honored the parameters in which they were given. I didn't want them to be taken away; in fact, I wanted even *more* privilege. I wanted to operate "Big Joe."

I worked on that ranch for six summers straight. The owner didn't let any of the teenagers operate his big backhoe, the one he called Big Joe. It was a crucial and very expensive piece of machinery on the ranch. If it were to break down, it would cost thousands of dollars to repair. The day came when I had finally proved myself worthy of trust and respect, because the owner offered to let me drive Big Joe. It was a golden moment that I remember vividly. Climbing up into that big black bucket seat, leering at those huge levers in front of me, was intimidating and exhilarating at the same time. As I started the engine and felt the rumble underneath me, I smiled so big I thought my heart would burst. This was it! I worked so hard, and here I was experiencing the one thing I set out to achieve! It was such a gratifying, powerful feeling.

Now, you may think this all sounds corny, but I believe the work ethic I developed as a teenager while working on the ranch has empowered me to be the strong, confident, successful businesswoman I am today.

Work Ethic Powered By Faith

I also believe it is incredibly important to have faith. Faith in something more powerful than yourself. Faith in what you're doing with your life. My personal belief system is that I am a child of God and He has a divine purpose for my life.

I fell in love very young, and got married to my best friend and soul mate when I was nineteen years old. We had a wonderful life filled with peace, joy, financial blessings, and healthy children. About ten years into our marriage, my husband began to get ill frequently. Five years later, he passed away, leaving me with two young girls to raise on my own. I'm sharing this with you because this event challenged my faith beyond anything I had ever experienced before. I stepped away from my faith because I didn't see God helping our situation at all. I later came back to my faith, because I quickly realized that life is full of heartache and disappointments, but if God is there with you through those trials, you aren't going through them alone. He has ultimate power; I don't. I *choose* daily to believe that God is good and He wants good for me. That doesn't mean bad things won't happen, but with God, I have hope.

It is through faith that I was called to build an augmented reality tech company. It is through faith that I stepped into the self-sacrificing role of an entrepreneur and trekked into the unknown realm of building a scalable business. It is through faith that I saturate my brain with as much knowledge as I can possibly fit in and surround myself with successful business mentors. It is through faith that I believe lives will be touched and positively changed because of my efforts. It is through faith in God's purpose for me that I persevere, and ultimately experience success. Faith plus hard work equals success.

Success for me is not monetary; that is a side effect. Success for me is knowing I'm living my life with purpose, and that purpose is to empower, enlighten, and encourage others to reach their success.

Michelle Calloway is a speaker, international bestselling author, and the founder and CEO of REVEALiO, Inc., an augmented reality marketing company. Michelle combines her expertise in visual communication with the emerging world of augmented reality, which overlays virtual content on top of real world objects, when they are viewed through a mobile smart device. It's amazingly connective technology. Her goal is to make these augmented reality experiences accessible and affordable for everyone, no matter the budget, to enhance relationships, gain influence, and increase revenue for business.

www.revealio.com

DON'T LET *THAT* STOP YOU

Judy Cook, MD

It used to bother me when people would say, "You're so lucky to be a doctor." They knew nothing of the obstacles and challenges starting very early in life that could easily have stopped me—especially the lack of family support. Fortunately I was very stubborn, and those few special people who believed in and encouraged me offset all the harsh criticisms from the family.

I grew up in an alcoholic family in the midst of lots of layers of dysfunction, so it's not too surprising that by the time I started elementary school, depression was already an all too familiar part of my life. However, talking about feelings was taboo, and even physical pain from a significant injury was never a justification for wanting sympathy or positive attention. My family did teach me, however, to be very analytical and find the flaws in almost anything and anyone, which especially included all *my* flaws. In my family, you had to be seriously sick to see a doctor, and help with how you might be feeling wasn't even a consideration.

Somehow, in the midst of all this, I decided quite early in life that I wanted to be a doctor and help people have a happier life. Why a doctor? Well, maybe it was related to that ongoing family "joke" about whether dad or mom's doctor had sired me, since at birth I was endowed with long black hair "just like the doctor's." Whether it was the "tale of two fathers," or the positive attention from my maternal grandmother on her all-too-rare visits, or support from doing well in school both from teachers and accomplishments such as being on the honor roll, somewhere, somehow I managed to find some sense of self-esteem and a willingness to stand up and fight. Being told that something I wanted to do "wasn't appropriate for a girl" had an effect much like waving a red flag in front of a bull!

To add to the stressors, in the middle of seventh grade, we moved from a tiny town in Minnesota to Houston, Texas. I was really an outcast there because I talked funny with my Minnesota accent, and I also promptly got labeled as a "brain"—one of those things that was "not ok for a girl" in the South. I did well in school and was the only National Merit Scholarship finalist in my class, but I did not get a scholarship. I was on the waiting list for Rice University, but I didn't get in, although four football players from my high school did—and three subsequently flunked out!

Although Mom and Dad had promised to send me to college, when the time came, they reneged on their promise—even though UT Austin was an inexpensive state school. *That* didn't stop me. Fortunately, Grandmother came through and helped things get started for college and guilt-tripped my parents into helping out a little while I worked part-time and went to school. My journey to a BS degree took seven years and included working in Austin while attending UT, a transfer to University of Houston so I could work on the COOP program with NASA, getting married, having a child, working at a Houston medical school, helping my husband through graduate school, and then divorcing him.

I continued working at the medical school after graduation. The job entailed getting specimens from the medical examiner's office for the research project I was involved in, and it also included the great blessing of being befriended there by a pathologist, Bob. He was very supportive of my curiosity about all things medical and the desire to be a doctor—which I still planned to do up to the time of the divorce. After my divorce, Bob and I were talking one day and he said, "OK, smarty, now that you are divorced, what are you going to do with yourself?"

I replied that I would probably work on a PhD degree because I didn't want to be someone's research technician for the rest of my life, but being a divorcee with a child was probably incompatible with going to medical school. His response was "You only have *one* child—don't let *that* stop you!"

I looked at him, stunned, and then told him the other problem was that I didn't have the money to go to medical school. His reply: "You focus on getting accepted and making passing grades, and they will find loan and scholarship money for you. Don't let *that* stop you! People don't get kicked out of medical school for lack of funds."

I timidly took the Medical College Aptitude Test (MCAT) and did well on it. Armed with those scores and good recommendations from faculty and the physicians I had worked for, I applied.

I was only accepted at one school, but it was a new school, with a younger, more open-minded faculty than most other schools. Off I went to medical school as a twenty-eight-year-old divorcee with a four-year-old child and not much money. The rest is history. Despite a lot of prejudice from some quarters, but blessed by considerable support from many others, I made it through. After doing a pathology residency, I realized psychiatry was where I belonged—and I finally also got the therapy I needed, which probably saved my life and certainly made me a better therapist. That has led to having a wonderful forty-year psychiatry career helping people have happier lives. It took a lot of effort to "get so lucky"!

Many obstacles will come along in your journey to your dreams, as they did in mine, but there will also be those giving support and encouragement to follow your dreams and desires. You have the choice to give up or to believe in yourself and those supporters so that you move forward and "don't let that stop you," no matter how tough "that" might be.

Dr. Judy Cook is a psychiatrist who has spent forty years utilizing primarily therapy to help many thousands of people heal their mental illness and change their lives for the better. These skills should not be reserved just for the mentally ill, because they can benefit all of us. Thus she has reinvented herself as a best-selling author, international speaker, coach, teacher, and trainer, which allows her to teach many more people the skills to be happier and more effective in all areas of their lives, whether as leaders, professionals, teachers, or family members.

www.GoDrJudy.com

YOU ARE RESPONSIBLE FOR YOUR LIFE

Kerri Courtright

Success is a real big word. I discovered that at the age of five.

While most kids liked to play with Barbies and color in coloring books, I enjoyed hanging out with the adults. I was an only child of two teenagers. The reason they married is pretty obvious. My parents were, and are, amazing. Back then they had nothing, and nothing is what I was used to. However, at the young age of five, I could see there were differences in my life versus the lives of others. My earliest recollection was waking up in my small bed. I later was informed that my bedroom was a closet in the one-bedroom apartment my parents shared.

When asked what I'd like to be when I grew up, I told people I wanted to be a lawyer. It was a lawyer who owned the biggest, most beautiful house on the lake where my grandparents had a small, two-bedroom cottage. It had a bathroom with a sink, toilet, and no shower. The lake was our bathtub.

A word I consistently heard growing up was no. No, you don't need that. No, we can't afford that. No, just because everyone else has that doesn't mean you need it. No, I'm sorry, you can only have one ballet class. No, we just don't have the money.

In fourth and fifth grade, kids called me "Kmart Kerri" since that was the only store my parents shopped at for all my clothes. Nicknames stay with you all your life; they can tear you down or be great motivators.

In life, you always have at least two choices. Either accept where you are and stay there, or change your course to where you want to go and become who you want to be. My desire at the age of five was to do whatever it took to have enough discretionary income to be able to have choices; though that might not have been my vocabulary at the time, it was my mentality. I wanted the ability to choose where I shopped, drink soda pop if I desired, or buy a car that didn't come with a rusted bottom.

My success story is that I became a "scrapper." It's a term of endearment to me. My husband likes to say that I "will" things to happen. So be it—I accept the words of affirmation. My motto was "whatever it takes."

In my teens, I was an independent contractor for fitness clubs. Making my own hours and setting my own wages was a thrilling new experience. This is how I paid my way through college. At the end of college, my boyfriend (soon to be husband) and I began our first company. It started with Ken selling signs and me making and shipping them.

We often worked through the night to make sure the signs were completed on time. This commitment meant many missed family functions and get-togethers with friends. This all paid off. Soon we had fantastic sales and our own manufacturing teams. Things were so good that we decided to widen our scope of business to include a passion. We loved to relax after work and watch movies in our living room, so we began opening video stores.

Things were great in the beginning. We had three fantastic video stores in great locations. Things were so good that even Blockbuster and Hollywood Video thought they could make some money. They set up a location one block from each of ours and their pockets were deeper than ours. To keep our video stores competing against the chain movie stores, we started taking money from the sign company to purchase more videos. The effort was good but, ultimately, we closed all video stores *and* the sign company.

Tangibly, we lost everything. Our employees, who believed in us, were out of jobs. We had no income. I was pregnant. My greatest fears of possibly losing our financial independence and having to raise my child under the financial stress that my parents raised me, was daunting. The years of "Kmart Kerri" came rushing to the forefront of my mind.

The thing is, though, what we lost were just tangible goods. We had learned what to do and what not to do. We discovered that we worked great together and could rely on each other. We knew that this was temporary and there was a much bigger plan for us.

When our businesses closed, we took time to regroup both as a couple and as business partners. Thinking through our business years, we realized that we had been giving out business tips to those who purchased signs from us. We made a pivot. The signs that were made for the business owners were just a part of helping them in their growth. There were other things that we could do to help them, expanding beyond the physical signs for their companies. Our business morphed into consulting. As time and techniques changed, we changed with them. When the Internet became user-friendly, we jumped in.

My husband and I now own TGC / Income Store, and today my wardrobe is filled with designer attire.

During all the early turmoil, we could have fought each other. We could have both gotten jobs. We could have . . .

Because I am a scrapper, I chose to fight. Our loss was just a temporary setback, something to learn from. It was simply time for a new goal.

It was a pivotal moment to realize how quickly things can change and the need to change with them.

The thing is . . . *the experiences of my youth became my fuel for success.*

It never crossed my mind to succumb and surrender. We all have choices. We can choose to fight for something or choose to fight to get away from something. Surrender is not an option. Each person has something amazing they are destined to do. Age and money are not prerequisites or limits.

Kerri Courtright is the co-founder of the Inc. 5000 company Income Store. Income Store helps people and businesses grow their income through building or buying revenue-generating websites.

Kerri runs Digital Footprint, their business growth conference that both Forbes and Inc. rank as one of the Top Five "Can't Miss" business conferences in North America.

Kerri, a former Chicago Bulls cheerleader, is now a best-selling author and elected official in Illinois.

After doubling revenues five years in a row (in 2013, 2015, 2016, and now again in 2017), their twenty-four-year-old company is ranked in Inc. magazine as one of the 1,000 Fastest Growing U.S. Companies.

www.IncomeStore.com

NEVER, NEVER, NEVER GIVE UP

Dr. Haleh Damavandi

The phone rang. I let it go to the answering machine because I was too afraid to speak to the doctor's office on the other end. I listened to the message left . . . a sweet voice identified herself as a nurse and asked that I please call their office as soon as possible. My heart started to race, and I felt sick to my stomach.

A month prior, my youngest son was getting ready to have his second major back surgery—only this time it was an emergency surgery. The titanium rod they had placed next to his spine to support his back six months before had snapped. My little nine-year-old boy was in excruciating pain, and all I could think about was how to help him. I would have done anything in the world for him . . . I would have given him my spine if I could have. Unfortunately the only option was another major surgery, this time putting in three titanium rods, taking one of his ribs out to use for bone, and fusing his spine. As any parent can imagine, I was distraught beyond belief.

At 8:00 a.m. my son was wheeled into the elevator to be taken in the operating room. While we were waiting for the elevator, my son's doctor looked over at me and asked in a quiet voice, "What is on your neck?" I was surprised by his question and did not really understand what he was asking. Then he pointed to my neck and told me I had a noticeable lump. I immediately responded with, "Oh, that's nothing . . . I'm just thin." The doctor gently touched my neck and told me that once my son came out of surgery and was home recovering, he wanted me to go to a doctor and have my neck checked. I replied, "Sure." That elevator ride felt like forever. All I could think about was my little boy; I didn't have the will or desire to think of my own health issue.

My son's surgery was a success, and after weeks in the hospital, he was finally able to come home. At my son's first checkup, the doctor immediately asked me if I followed up regarding my neck. I told him I had not for several reasons—all good ones, I thought, but he did not! He explained the seriousness of the issue, and I promised him I would get a checkup. I went to my doctor a week later and was told all I would need was a simple biopsy. I finally completed the procedure and was informed that based on everything it looked good and there was only a 5 percent chance I had cancer. I was so happy to hear those odds! After weeks of waiting to get the results, the day finally came. I was already under enough stress caring for my sweet little boy recovering from back surgery. I just wanted to hear the good news that it was nothing and move on in life.

I finally got up the courage to call my doctor's office. I kept telling myself not to worry; I was young, only thirty-eight years old. I took care of myself, I worked out (for goodness sakes, I was even a black belt in karate), I ate healthy food, and I didn't smoke! What more could anyone do to maintain their health? It *had* to be good news.

The doctor came on the line and said, "I have your results." There was a slight pause, and then he said, "Unfortunately, it's cancer."

I felt my knees go weak as I slid down the wall to the floor. I told him it had to be a mistake, to which he replied, "I'm sorry, but it's not."

A few weeks passed. I finally accepted the facts and made a decision to fight like never before and live life to the fullest no matter what the outcome. After surgery, radiation, and other treatments over the years, I finally reached my ten-year cancer-free mark, which felt like freedom from the chains of cancer.

Looking back, I've wondered how I was able to overcome the many challenges I have faced in my life. One of the first decisions I had made was to finish my education. It was a very long process to complete my doctorate in psychology. Along the way I lost both of my parents (one to suicide and one to cancer), went through a divorce, moved across the country for my son to be treated by the best doctor, raised three young boys as a single mom, went to school, worked—and built a successful business.

I believe that every day in life we are performing—to what degree is the big question. Personally, I aspire to be the best I can be with whatever I am doing, which is how I was able to overcome challenges and accomplish what I have in life. My life lessons helped me define the work I do, specializing in performance psychology, which I love. I am extremely passionate about helping others overcome obstacles and achieve their dreams.

We all have those moments when we think about things we would like to accomplish and dreams we would like to fulfill, but unfortunately we put it off to another day due to many different reasons. We can find several excuses for "why" we are not reaching our goals or following our dreams, such as telling ourselves we don't have the time, money, resources, or support—or possibly we even have a health crisis . . . they all sound like legitimate reasons. Well, I think that is all BS! We need to get out of our own way and set our lives on fire so we can maximize our potential in life! Otherwise, we are just fooling ourselves. Ask yourself, "If not now . . . when?" You *can* do anything you put your mind to!

Dr. Haleh Damavandi is a leading international expert in the field of performance psychology. She has worked with world-class athletes, elite military, performing artists, and leading business executives. Dr. Haleh helps them overcome mental, emotional, and physical obstacles to take their performance to the next level. Dr. Haleh developed a brain/body technique, SOAR (self, optimization, awareness, release), that yields great success in helping individuals unlock their blocks to achieve optimal performance in any area of life. Dr. Haleh is honored to work with and give back to the military and their families. She is also the proud mother of three amazing young men.

DoctorHaleh@gmail.com

WHAT THE FOOK!

Lorna Day

Would you believe that a person who hates to cook could actually pen a cookbook? Well, that is exactly what has happened, and that journey now has led me into writing about food, which I absolutely love. The more I write and experiment, the more opportunities arise, such as judging local food-centric events.

I believe that everything we go through in life can be a key ingredient to finding our purpose. I hated cooking. It was tedious and intricate and sometimes, after all that work, it still didn't come out right; I would blame Martha, Julia, and Betty. I would look at recipes and say to myself, "Why not just add this?" or " Why go through all of those steps; just change this."

Sounds easy right? The problem was that I was twenty-six years old and had just opened a 150-seat restaurant with no kitchen experience. Even after hiring chefs, I eventually ended up in the kitchen, and I secretly started taking shortcuts with recipes to make them easier—and to my surprise our guests loved the food! I was flabbergasted at first. I felt like a fraud because I did not have the schooling or the experience to be warranting such amazing responses for my creations.

I was in a very abusive relationship at the time. The lack of confidence in both my professional and personal life caused me to become sick, and I eventually lost the restaurant. It was one of the hardest things I have ever dealt with. I fought for seven years for my restaurant, The Metro Blues Café, which was one of the best in town. I eventually hired a manager to help with the day-to-day, and he chose to steal my money. I was so devastated when I found out! I trusted him; I felt it was unfair; I said, "Why me" to everyone; it was horrible. I was forced to claim bankruptcy and close the restaurant.

After several months of feeling sorry for myself, I woke up with an epiphany: I could not have learned more about business if I had went to Harvard. Freedom was in front of me, and I have never looked back. I was a single mom with two children to support, so I started a lunch account out of my house. I literally started by picking up the phonebook and calling old clients from the restaurant as well as some people I didn't know. I just knew that once I fed them they would be hooked. I did this for several years until I could afford a commercial kitchen.

Having the commercial kitchen was wonderful, but the costs were high, so I applied the same concept of looking at what I perceived as a negative and figuring out how could I make it a positive. Since I had the commercial space and was struggling to pay the rent, I wondered if there were other businesses like mine who were working from their homes because they couldn't afford to do it any other way. I called a few smaller companies, and lo and behold, they were open, receptive, and thankful that I was willing to open my kitchen up to them at a shared cost. Not only did I alleviate my financial stress by sharing my kitchen, it actually became profitable for me. I was so thrilled with how this process of finding positives was working that I just kept applying it.

My biggest breakthrough was the most obvious to everyone but myself: teaching cooking and writing a cook book. You see, to me I was still that girl who didn't have the right culinary schooling; I still felt like a fraud even though people were raving after every event.

I started teaching classes, groups of fifteen or twenty, usually consisting of my clients. I was thrilled and honored to be teaching. One day I invited a friend of mine to attend a class. It was a Greek class, and we were all dressed in toga gear, except my friend. She sat through the class, thanked me at the end, and then left.

I was cleaning up when my phone rang; it was my friend. I was expecting her to thank me for inviting her, but instead she said, "What the f@#K are you doing? You are in front of twenty people who know, like, and love you, and you are wasting your time. You need to be in front of thousands—you have the 'it factor' to make it big, and I can't stand seeing you play so small."

My jaw dropped. I didn't know what to say, so I said nothing. I actually wanted to cry because I was hurt by her response. I muttered something, and we hung up. It wasn't till the next day that I realized she was right. If I applied that same positive principal to my food, what could I create? Instantly the word *fooking* (fun + cooking= fooking) popped into my head. So I hadn't been schooled in cooking, but damn, I created Fooking!

I looked back at all the recipes I changed, the sauces I created, the steps I ignored, and the fear of being a fraud, and I realized it was all in alignment with me getting people to stop cooking and start "fooking." I had just been on the phone with a guy and we were discussing fooking, and he said, "My girlfriend and I love to eat, but we hate to cook." The next day I heard the same sentiment from yet another young man.

We call it the LTEHTC (love to eat, hate to cook) Syndrome. I took a foodie leap of faith and wrote my book, *The Fook Book: Untraditional Recipes for Sexy People*. It is about reclaiming your power in the kitchen, dominating your dishes, and being confident—all with a smile. In closing, question everything! At some point in history, someone decided how most things are accomplished, and I like to think we can all challenge that.

As a saucy cocktail waitress on a quest for world domination, Lorna Day never dreamed she'd land in the kitchen, but that is just what happened when she opened her first restaurant, The Metro Blues Café. Hating to cook herself, Lorna trusted her instincts and started revamping recipes to create easy versions. Unknowingly she had started to fook.

Now a successful business owner, caterer, columnist, food critic and author, she's been crowned the Fooking Queen of Innovative Eating. Her dirty little secret? She's never been professionally trained, which means she's not required to play by the same old boring rules. Lorna's delicious, simple recipes prove that with some culinary balls and a cocktail in your hand, cooking can be fun, fearless, fast, and fabulous.

"I feel people have turned to convenience foods because they think cooking at home is anything but convenient," says Lorna, "but fooking is the five-star version of wham, bam, thank you, ma'am!"

Lorna Day lives in Stuart, Florida, with her two children, Remington and Christina; four dogs, Eggs, Herford, China Bell, and Marcy. She is the owner of Ooo La La Catering and Island Rose Catering, the author of The Fook Book: Untraditional Recipes for Sexy People. *She also pens* Edible Oohs and Ahhs *for* Stuart Magazine *and dining reviews for* Stuart Living Magazine.

lorna@ooolalalife.com
www.letsfook.com

WHEN PRINCE CHARMING ISN'T COMING

Susan DeRobertis

Things happen in life that you can't plan for; it's the unimaginable happening. And when that life-turning event happens, everything changes. It could be a divorce, a death, a bankruptcy, or some other event that cuts you to the core, and your world gets upended.

For me, it was divorce.

My divorce ripped me to my core. Although I still loved my husband, the resentment and constant compromising over the years took its toll. At year ten, when our friends were renewing their vows, I thought to myself, "Would I marry him again and say yes?" I knew then what the answer was, and I wasn't ready or willing to face my truth. Instead I told myself "things will change"—for another five years! It took everything I had inside me one night to tell my husband that I couldn't do it anymore. It had taken many years before the pain finally outweighed my fear.

My life changed in the few moments it took to express what had been there for years. It felt as though I was in the *Harry Potter* movie where the stairs realigned, changing the look and outcome of everything. And yes, it was terrifying. And exhilarating! I had finally put myself first and stepped outside my marriage.

Amazingly, the courage it took to free myself drew other women to me, asking me how I did it. Out of that conversation, my coaching business, Venus in Transit, was born! That was truly a gift because it changed the course of my career. I had studied accounting and business in college and worked my way up the ladder to controller and later CFO. After some mergers and acquisitions, I left the concept of working for someone behind and created my own accounting business for small business owners and entrepreneurs.

My business was good until my divorce hit, and then my income took a deep dive.

Financial Success Is a Rite of Passage into Your Power

Although I was an accountant and the CEO of my own business, I was a mess when it came to taking care of me financially—even though I knew numbers, math, statistics, finance, and spreadsheets! I could take care of accounting clients of all kinds with all types of businesses, figure out how to increase their income, reduce their expenses, get more clients, and create different streams of income for them. But when it came to me, I blanked out and my eyes rolled to the back of my head.

How could this be? I was a woman, after all. Women and money make strange partners.

It comes down to the hard-wiring. Sometimes you have to fail so you can succeed. I know I did.

After my divorce, I carried the mortgage on our house myself. Between taxes, upkeep, and the real estate market taking a dive in 2008, I didn't reap the profits I anticipated when I wanted to sell. My business also took a big hit as half of my clients went out of business. For the next few years, to make ends meet I lived on credit cards and cashed in my IRAs. I saw everything I had built be washed away. I had no safety net. All I had was me.

So there I was, seventy-five thousand dollars in credit card debt, and making 30 percent of what was once a profitable accounting business. My fledgling coaching business, Venus in Transit, was not enough to support me yet either.

No one knew what was going on in my life.

I was ashamed of the debt, ashamed of not being responsible with money, and thinking things would change but not doing anything different! Even though I never missed a payment, never defaulted on loans, always paid the mortgage on time, I judged myself and felt inferior.

What had to change was me. I realized that doing nothing was a decision, and taking the same actions would get me the same results. So I chose to do something different.

I asked for help.

Not long after that I hired a financial planner and began a new chapter in my life of creating wealth and financial security. This was the turning point.

I knew in my heart I was meant to teach and lead; this had always been my passion. But as an adult, it's hard to lead when your life is a financial mess, especially if you're a money coach. It seemed like a cruel joke. Money was the one constant I struggled with; I never made enough money to live the life I wanted once I was divorced.

The difference showed up when I changed my relationship to myself rather than trying to change everything *outside* myself. Rather than doing and running and taking on everything imaginable, I stopped and sat down. I stood still. I was with me—just me. And in that following year I doubled my income.

What really changed was my view of who I am. I had thought of myself as something that was broken and needed fixing. I loathed myself and my inability to make my life work. While I had immense compassion for others who suffered, I had none for myself. I was judgmental and impatient and viewed myself as a failure.

But then I realized how strong I was, courageous in the face of my own worst enemy—myself. My resilience and persistence paid off, and I realized I had everything I needed to create *anything* I wanted all the time. My manifestation talents were intact and ready to be called upon.

We can't do it alone. Everyone needs support, guidance, and yes, even love from those who have walked that walk. The very thing we mess up and struggle with is where our gold is hidden. Think of the grain of sand that irritates the oyster until it becomes a pearl. My mess, my grain of sand, was money, and that's how it manifested materially because the real issue was below the surface. Money is not just paper to get us stuff. It's energy. It's an exchange that points to your self-worth and self-love. When you're on the other side of it, you can feel quite humble and grateful. Gratitude is something I'm conscious of on a daily basis now.

Take stock, look around at all the goodness in your life, and be grateful. Gratitude is the cornerstone in creating a life filled with abundance, love, and prosperity. True wealth lies in the quality of your relationships and the difference you make in the world.

My life now is a constant adventure; I'm live continually in a state of wonder, love, and fun. I'm always tuned in and always turned on.

And grateful for it all.

Susan De Robertis is a transformation and empowerment coach, motivational speaker, and writer. Susan's mission is to teach women to live life on purpose, have the confidence and clarity to claim their voice, and create financial freedom and fulfillment. Susan believes that when a woman is empowered, she transforms her life and is able to make better decisions for herself.

www.susanderobertis.com

WHAT DO YOU WANT TO BE WHEN YOU GROW UP?

Giovanna Dottore

"A whale trainer!" That's what I would say when someone asked, "What do you want to be when you grow up?"

Politely they would reply, "Oh." But the look on their face was akin to a dog tilting its head to say, "Huh?"

"You know, the person in the wetsuit who trains Shamu at Sea World."

"Oh! You want to do that?"

Yes, I wanted to do that. Nearly every school project through my first twelve years of school involved whales or dolphins. In fifth grade we had Whale Day. We transformed the playground into a whale educational activity center and hosted tours for each of the other classes to enjoy. In high school I made a connection with one of the educators in Sea World's education center, and he sent materials for my projects and answered my litany of questions. I had a clear vision of myself wearing that red wetsuit and playing with Shamu in front of hundreds of spectators.

During my senior year of high school, I received a packet from Sea World's education department with all the classes and experience needed to become a whale trainer—more accurately, a marine biologist. I couldn't wait to open the packet. I stood in the doorway of my closet carefully reading the material. There were pages and pages of classes that ended in "-ology." I was starting to lose interest. Between that and the number of years required as an apprentice and the experience needed in public speaking, I decided that being a whale trainer was not for me.

I now found myself, after twelve years, with no idea of what I wanted to be "when I grow up," and college was only a few months away. Growing up at that time, there was still a bit of a traditional mind-set that you study, get a job, work hard, and retire from the same place you started. I never heard guidance counselors say that it was possible to have multiple interests and careers. Which made it even more daunting to settle on *one*

—what if it wasn't the right one? Would I be stuck? Could I change to something else?

I worked in the funeral industry for a few hours after school, but I didn't see any potential for me there. I was fascinated by those who were clear on what they wanted and were declaring majors. On my first day of college, I still wasn't sure, so I focused on general education. I felt the pressure of what I was going to do *after* college. What did I want for a career? Where did I want to work? I wanted to take a variety of classes, but I also wanted to graduate on time. I completed all the general ed classes—time to decide. I settled on marketing. It seemed like a skill that could be used in a variety of industries and transferrable to just about anywhere. I spent the next two years understanding the ins and outs of the four Ps: price, place, product, and promotion, as well as changing brand image and leading project teams to run companies and internships. I did well, but was I supposed to do this for the rest of my life?

I later landed a job at a major toy company . . . in logistics. Not much marketing in that role, but I did have a blast with the toys. I was discovering that maybe I wasn't meant to do only one thing. I had a thirst to learn and was energized to start on new projects. One of my employees asked me, "Do you mind if I ask how old you are—because you sure know a lot, but you don't look old enough."

Then one day I heard a thought-provoking question. I was a speaker coach for a TEDx youth event, and one of the high school speakers delivered a powerful speech on "What If We Weren't Meant to Do Just One Thing?" It was an a-ha moment for me. By that time I had already worked in five different departments (none were marketing per se), competed successfully in West Coast Swing dancing, was elected to the highest district position in Toastmasters, and was ready for the next challenge. Since then I've been in two more roles at work, became a leadership trainer, designed award-winning newsletters, trained church lectors, helped groups improve their work processes, raised over $18K in charitable toy drives—and I still don't know what I want to be when I grow up. I'm now exploring voice-over acting.

When I finally let go of the worry of changing careers and interests, I began to explore more and enjoy having a diverse background and a wealth of experiences. It was leverage—not undecisiveness. It sets me up to take on any situation and demonstrates the value I can bring to an organization or team. We don't know what the future holds. My early days of logistics, merchandising, and account planning prepared me for running the company's national retail outlets, which helped me oversee the Toastmasters district, which helped me navigate teams, budgets, and workshop facilitation, which has helped me in setting up personal businesses, and so much more.

I remember the first time I was asked, "What would you do if you knew you wouldn't fail?" I said I would have a company called "Low Hanging Fruit" that helps small businesses tackle the obvious-but-sometimes-overlooked opportunities to improve their business. It's still on my radar, but I have a few other things I want to do first.

"Be anything you want to be; do what you want to do" is not a new message. However, I think it's an important reminder that rather than stressing over the one thing you "need" to become or worry about whether you change your mind, it's OK and valuable to enrich your life with many things. As I once learned, "Sometimes you have to give up the things you have to have what you don't."

What do *you* want to be when you grow up?

Giovanna Dottore has been in the toy industry for eighteen-plus years and plays on one of the world's biggest playgrounds. She led the merchandising efforts for boys brands on the Walmart account, was charged with lean process improvement for logistics, ran their retail outlet business in the U.S., managed supply chain organizational development, and is an MBA intern mentor. She combines her business background with her thirst for training and facilitation. A philanthropist, her annual toy drive, Joy Through Toys, promotes play and imagination among children. Giovanna is a Toastmasters Past District Governor—ranked ninth out of 82 global districts, a 2013 TEDxYouth@Bommer Canyon conference speaker-coach, and the 2002 U.S. Open Advanced Strictly Swing Dance champion. She dabbles in voice-over work.

www.giovannadottore.com

FIGHTING THE GOOD FIGHT OF FAITH

Vivian R. England

There was a time when things in my life began to become topsy-turvy. I had been going through spiritual warfare on the job for years; I suffered a miscarriage, which almost took my mind. Then my marriage began to fall apart, after my mother-in-law passed away, having been married to her son for only four years. It was as if the man I married died with his mother, because he completely shut down. There was no more communication between us, or if there was any, it was very limited. Yet when he got around his friends, especially in the church, he seemed to come alive.

As time progressed, matters seemed to get worse. My husband became more distant, until I felt as though I only had a roommate. I was being attacked from the left and the right. Every day I would go into my private chambers and war against the enemy through prayer. Spirits of depression, anxiety, and low self-esteem tried to attach themselves to me and hurl me into a state of bondage. One day the Lord awakened me and told me that it wasn't anything wrong with me; it was something wrong with my husband. He could not go where the Lord was carrying me. Those words of the Lord gave me comfort and peace of mind. The enemy became defeated!

My mind reflected back on how many times the enemy tried to take my life. At the age of three months, I was plagued with chicken pox from one of my older siblings. My mother tells me I had such a terrible bout, I almost died—defeated. At the age of five months, another older sibling had a pillow and was just getting ready to smother me when my mother entered the room just in the nick of time—defeated. On another occasion, while I was sitting in my walker, my mother happened to enter the room and that same sibling had placed a diaper over my head, still trying to smother me—defeated.

Later, in the eighth grade, I found myself in an altercation at school that resulted in my getting stitches in the back of my head. One of my

71

classmates went around telling people she was going to come to school the next day to kick my butt. Why? To this day, it is beyond my comprehension. However, during the altercation, the children in the class said, "Uh, oh, she's got a knife!" My mind went through this dialogue: "What are they talking about? I don't have a knife. Oh, *she's* got a knife! Well, you better get the best of her." It seemed like the two of us had been fighting for quite some time. Finally, my teacher pulled me from off the top of her. The girl jumped up and headed straight for the door. The teacher summoned her back, but she refused and proceeded out the door. He turned to me and said, "You're cut. I'm taking you down to the nurse's office."

As we were walking down the hallway, I felt something trickling down the back of my head. When I drew my hand back, there was blood on my fingers. I stated, "She cut me in the back of my head." Arriving at the nurse's office, she accessed the situation and indicated that I needed stitches. My mother came to the school and drove me to George Washington Hospital (GW). At GW, the nurse prepped the area and the doctor sutured the area. When he was finished, the doctor said, "You are lucky, young lady! If it was an inch deeper, you would have died." I don't believe in luck, I believe in God! The enemy was defeated once again. Hallelujah!

Know that the enemy will use anyone—whether foe or family—to try and take us out. However, the Bible says:

Finally, my brethren, be strong in the Lord, and in the power of His might. Put on the whole armour of God, that ye may be able to stand against the wiles of the devil. For we wrestle not against flesh and blood, but against principalities, against powers, against the rulers of the darkness of this world, against spiritual wickedness in high places. (Ephesians 6:10–12, KJV)

It is never the individual that we are warring against; we are in a constant spiritual warfare. However, we can always come out victoriously if we keep the faith and hold to God's unchanging hand. Hebrews 11:1 says, "Now faith is the substance of things hoped for, the evidence of things not seen."

"Now faith is" is expressing a fact about the present, whereas "of things hoped for" is directed toward the future. So according to this Scripture, we can safely say that the things we hope to possess in the future are brought nigh by our present faith. Our present faith will bring a manifestation of the invisible things not yet seen.

No matter what happens in your life, hold on to your faith in God! If you don't have a relationship with Him, get to know Him. Romans 8:28

says, "And we know that all things work together for good to them that love God, to them who are the called according to His purpose."

Everyone on the face of this earth was born with a purpose. It doesn't matter whether your mother's pregnancy was planned or not; God has a plan for your life. No one can fulfill that plan except you. Get in the Word of God and develop a relationship with Him through prayer and His Word. Ask Him, "God, what is the plan for my life?"

God revealed to me His plan for my life. That's why I fight the good fight of faith, against all odds. Before leaving this earth, I aim to fulfill my purpose. I encourage you to do the same. Fight the good fight of Faith!

Vivian R. England—The Voice of Inspiration—is a native Washingtonian, an international speaker, author, sign language interpreter, community advocate, spiritual counselor, and ordained minister. She has a passion for the Deaf, seniors, young children, single mothers, and those less fortunate. Having survived many setbacks in life, her mission is to reach out to help other hurting women. Her desire is to let them know they can rise above the pain, hurt, and agony to embrace a newfound love, joy, and peace that lies within. Her contact information is: P.O. Box 7137, Largo, MD 20792.

living4purpose@yahoo.com

GETTING OFF THE WORRY-GO-ROUND

Linda Fostek

I like the merry-go-round. Now, don't laugh. It's true. The steed you choose and where you choose to sit on the merry-go-round says a lot about you and your life. Do you choose to ride inside, safe and slow, where your view is obstructed, or are you on the outside, moving fast where you can see everything as it passes you by? Is your horse stationary and secure, or does it move up and down, requiring you to hold on tight? Are you reaching for the gold ring as you whirl around on your painted pony? Do you grab for it, again and again, each time reaching out a little further? If you get one ring, do you stop grabbing for another? Is one enough?

The merry-go-round is a giant metaphor for life.

2017 dawned, a year full of hopes and dreams. A new life-supporting machine sat between my husband and me in the den. Fully trained, I was his care-partner in Home Hemo-Dialysis. After two-and-a-half years of in-center treatment that sapped his energy and stole his life, we had transitioned to treatment at home.

He felt better than he had in years and was enjoying life again. He was even writing a cookbook. The time we spent together during treatment was a time to talk, laugh, and just enjoy being together.

I was gearing up for an exciting year in my business too. Book sales and speaking opportunities were filling my calendar. I was networking a lot, expanding my relationships with those I met as clients, resources, and referrals. The busy expo season was nearly upon me when, in March, my husband ended up in the hospital.

In that moment, my merry-go-round turned into a worry-go-round.

My husband's health had been fragile for years. I was used to dealing with his health issues. But nothing had prepared me for the journey we were about to take. The IV antibiotics used to treat an infection caused a horrific adverse drug event called Steven Johnson's Syndrome. His entire epidermis blistered and peeled from his knees down. It looked as though he had been severely burned. Because of his compromised health with diabetes and kidney failure, he was unable to recover. Over the next three months, secondary infection, gangrene, and sepsis followed.

On May 31st my sweet, loving Gentle Giant, my once strong 6'8" husband of twenty-six years transitioned from this life to the next. He did so, both of us at peace, without fear and without worry.

How did I get off the worry-go-round and get back on the merry-go-round of my life?

I had been my husband's caregiver; there was no one else, no children, just me. I was also an entrepreneur with a growing business to run. I knew how gravely ill he was, and I knew that someday I would need to be able to take care of myself. I would escape to networking events two or three times a week. That three-hour distraction was focused on others and my business and was essential to my well-being. I didn't bring what I was dealing with at home to those meetings. I was living in the moment, recharging my batteries. Those escapes allowed me to be the attentive, loving caregiver I wanted to be. It was essential to my survival during this time and set me up for the things that would follow.

It's interesting that when a loved one is sick for a long time, you grieve the loss of each function and ability together as it occurs. You laugh, you cry, and you share the journey together. In the end, when your loved one is released from their suffering and pain, so are you.

The irony of it all is that my business, The Crisis Planner, was focused on being prepared for the disasters of life. The planning systems in my two books, *And Now What?* and *Shit Happens,* worked seamlessly and helped me navigate through the grieving process.

It was time to get off the inside horse on my merry-go-round. It was time for me to ride the outside steed—the one with the flared nostrils, wild mane, and brightly painted saddle. It was time for me to grab that golden ring. With focused determination, my eyes wide open, that is exactly what I did.

The first golden ring I grabbed was an opportunity to be part of Awakening Giants San Diego, a journey that would challenge me physically, emotionally, spiritually, personally, and professionally. I would take on a High-Ropes course, sleep with wolves at The Wolf Connection, take part in an Amazing Race, meet Don Miguel Ruiz (author of *The Four Agreements*), and deliver an Inspire Talk. I would laugh, cry, and grow stronger than I ever thought possible.

As the merry-go-round came around again, I grabbed another golden ring: speaking on the stage at the 10th Annual Women's Prosperity

Network Un-Conference in Orlando. My Topic: Get Off the Worry-Go-Round with The Crisis Planner.

I captured a third golden ring as an international speaker on Sharon Frame's LeadHERShip Cruise. I had been invited to speak on networking, a topic I lived every day in my business. Four weeks before the cruise, Sharon asked if I had published any blogs or white papers on networking. I responded, "Not yet, but I can work on it."

What came out of that inquiry has surprised even me. Within two weeks I had written a new book, Love/Hate Networking: The Essential Guide to Getting a BIG ROI from Networking (Even If You Hate It). The book launched on December 13, and is now an Amazon best seller, my fourth golden ring.

On December 29, I was named 2017 Networker of the Year by 516/631 Ads, a prominent Long Island networking resource for ring number five. The networking side of my business is taking on a life of its own, with speaking and workshop events.

Five golden rings.

I'm reaching for more, how about you?

Are you ready to get off your worry-go-round?

Linda Fostek is an international speaker, author, and consultant on a mission to empower others to get off the worry-go-round and become their own Master of Disaster. Linda knows first-hand how preparation and planning allows companies and individuals to navigate through and thrive when blindsided by life. Linda brings her expertise, kind heart and compassion together guiding others through planning for the inevitable disasters be they personal or natural. Inspired by her late father, Norbert Osiecki, Linda, carries on his legacy through her recent books And Now What? *and* Shit Happens. *Her passion for networking resulted in the release of her Amazon bestselling book* Love/Hate Networking *and being named 2017 Networker of the year by 516/631 Ads, a prominent Long Island Networking resource.*

Linda is the co-leader of two chapters of Women's Prosperity Network, Certified Speaker, and member of The One Philosophy Founders Circle.

www.TheCrisisPlanner.com

EPIPHANY IN NEPAL AND TIBET

Patricia Karen Gagic

Standing alone in what is known as the "Roof of the World" and "The Third Pole" was a dream come true.

In 2015 a small group of people were invited by Lama Glenn Mullin, one of the world's leading Tibetologists, published Buddhist author, international lecturer, teacher, and translator of classical Tibetan literature and historical ancient art, to join him on a sacred pilgrimage to Nepal and Tibet. I was one of the lucky invited guests.

After reading the itinerary, which was nothing short of an extreme adventure, my mind raced ahead. Nepal had experienced a devastating earthquake in the southern Himalayas a few months earlier that had created not only architectural damage and loss of life, but also a massive impact on the economy. My decision to go became even more important from a humanitarian perspective. Diving deep into my intuition, I knew the Universe had singled me out for this privilege. We would offer moral support to those who felt abandoned, neglected, and challenged. It would be meaningful to see foreigners help restore a sense of balance and support.

Preparing oneself physically, mentally, and spiritually for this incredible journey required a long pause into facing my own fears. Of the several I felt might impede my ability to participate, my physical limitation was primary. The itinerary was carefully crafted as a sacred pilgrimage that included daily mile-long hikes in very deserted areas in high altitude. Just reading those words brought on anxiety. After spending time reading as much as possible and being in discussion with the tour organizer and Lama Glenn, I achieved a greater sense of confidence. I was now on a mission!

Landing in Kathmandu, my heart was filled with excitement and an inner knowing that everything would be perfect, and it was. There were so many extraordinary, magical and precious moments, that I felt as though I were floating twenty-four hours a day. My eyes never closed as the sights and sounds were so breathtaking and unfamiliar. The damaged roads and buildings screamed for healing. The night sounds of barking dogs were never-ending. Displaced animals fought for food and territory and lived on the ruptured streets laden with rocks and debris. Each day as we visited the temples and monasteries, we were always greeted by beautiful and engaging locals who smiled shyly as they acknowledged our presence. It was very humbling to witness.

Our group bonded and became a family. As we meandered across Nepal and Tibet, hiking into sacred caves, bathing in mystical waters, and chanting with monks and nuns, we realized that there is no such thing as fear. In fact, the lessons had been perfectly aligned for each of us. There is no shortage of beauty in simply "being" when you are immersed in places where achieving enlightenment and living in complete mindfulness and awareness clothes both your mind and heart. We spent hours together, reading, talking, and meditating—fueling our energy for the next day's adventure.

I recall one significant afternoon in the Chimpuk Mountains near Lhasa. Everyone had a personal desire to either reach, see, or experience something unique. The visit to the caves is a tough walk. I had followed Lama Glenn and another guest to a very beautiful cave, where I chose to rest after a good two-mile hike. They decided to continue up to another cave. It might have been the altitude (over 14,000 feet) which contributed to my calmness and comfort when I parked myself on a large rock outside the opening of several well-adorned cave entrances. Several minutes passed, and I could hear shuffling sounds coming up behind me. A herd of mountain sheep, a few yaks, and several nuns in their long robes nodded and continued along the undefined path. I looked down at my walking shoes, which were filled with yak dung, and breathed a sigh of relief, exalting with great pride how I had "made it."

I closed my eyes and reveled in the thought of how extraordinary it was to be thousands of miles away from home, surrounded by nature without a drop of fear in my mind. Seconds later I was startled to find a very old monk standing in front me, grinning from ear to ear. He was the "gatekeeper of the cave" and probably had lived there for more than fifty or sixty years.

This moment was frozen in time. We literally stared at each other in amusement. I was wearing my Prada sunglasses, carrying a walking stick, a knapsack, and in full makeup. He spoke no English, and I did not speak any Tibetan. I suddenly wished Lama Glenn was walking back down the mountain! The monk seemed amused at my casualness (and probably my clothes!). After a staring contest which lasted at least four minutes, he scurried away, returning moments later with a handful of cookies, candies, and a pillow, which he gestured for me to sit on. I'm pretty sure this was a pillow circa 1950 and probably never had been sat on by anyone but him—and now me. I was incredibly humbled—and I was becoming a bit nervous, too, as it was late afternoon and I had a long walk down the mountain alone. Without hesitation the monk moved toward my face, removed my sunglasses, and put them on! I took a picture with my phone and showed it to him. He again grinned and held me in his gaze for what seemed a very long time. It was a supernatural moment. I caught myself wondering if this was really happening or was it some kind of a vision?

As I ventured down the mountain, wild animals, birds, and flowers completed the ambient trek. Fear vanished and a oneness I had never before experienced in my life appeared. Epiphany.

Patricia Karen Gagic is an international contemporary artist, the award-winning author of Karmic Alibi and Karma and Cash, and the co-author of several books. She was recognized by WXN Women's Executive Network as one of the TOP 100 Most Powerful Women in Canada in 2015, 2016, and 2017. She was knighted by the International Order of St. George in 2013 and was the recipient of the Canadian Civil Liberties Association Award in 2017. She is a graduate of the University of Toronto, Faculty of Social Work in Applied Mindfulness and Transformative Mindfulness as a trained meditation specialist. She is a Reiki master, Feng Shui consultant, member of the Ontario Cabinet for Friends of the Canadian Museum for Human Rights, and member of the Sir Edmund Hilary Board of Directors. She is actively involved with Project Cambodia and Hearts Healing Humanity.

www.patriciakarengagic.com
www.inspiredtoberewired.com

TUNE IN, TELL THE TRUTH,
AND PASS IT ON!

Mary Anne Kurzen

"Ms. Kurzen, thank God you're here," my eleventh grade Life Skills student Omar shouted, jumping over the guardrail around the bungalow and racing through the open door of my classroom after school one day. "I need you to take off tomorrow, Ms. Kurzen, so you can go to court with me and be my lawyer!"

I had shared with my class that I actually had several law classes under my belt and had been planning to become an attorney for troubled teens. But though I loved the intellectual stimulus of the classes, when I checked my priorities, I decided to become a teacher and help kids decide *not* to get into trouble!

"You were absent today, and . . ."

"I was in court, and my parents won't pay for a lawyer—this is bad. What am I supposed to do?"

Convinced that no teacher can be truly successful without Divine Inspiration, I took a deep breath and asked for inner guidance. Then it hit me!

"Oh my gosh, Omar, that was *you* yesterday, wasn't it? You were driving around, circling the school in a brand-new, enormous, shiny white SUV, bumping 'Ghetto Rap,' right?"

He came clean right away. "Yes, and . . ."

I let go and turned inward. Suddenly yesterday's loud, music-blasting car scenario flashed before my eyes. "Omar! You stole that car!" I shrieked.

"Well not really . . . I . . . I just . . ."

"Borrowed it!" I filled in for him.

"Well, I was just gonna roll around the school and drive it back, but now supposubly . . ."

"Supposubly? *Supposedly?*" I mulled the word over in my mind, as the imagined news flash in my awareness continued to unfold. *Hmm, what could be worse than just stealing—yes, it was stealing, even if, as Omar says, the lady left the keys in the car. . . .* My hunch was right. It was at the convenience store just down the road.

"OMG! Omar, you stole a car from out in in front of the 7-Eleven—close enough to whiz around the school, looking cool, blasting some raps, and then you could have the rig back before the lady came out of the store, but . . . there was a *kid* in the back seat?

". . . who woke up and grabbed me around the neck from behind!" Omar continued my thread. "Man! I nearly got into an accident!"

"So now you are also accused of grand theft auto—and kidnapping!"

"Right, but I didn't mean to do it!"

"But, Omar, your actions show that is indeed what happened."

"Now what do I do? Ms. Kurzen, you are so smart. You are the smartest person I know—what do we do?"

Well, thanks for the accolade, kid, and what's with the "we"? I thought, but this was no time to be snide. Omar had walked into my room, seeking help, and I stay focused. No blaming or complaining was going to remedy the situation. I glanced at the stack of essays on my desk needing to be graded, but Omar was my project for today. *Think, teacher, think.*

Suddenly I had a thought. I raced over to my desk and checked my roll book. "Great! I was right—you are still seventeen! Good news! Okay, Omar, God is on your side."

"Okay, thank you, God," he said absently, looking at the ceiling, "But what do I do?"

"Well, you start by telling the truth! Omar, you square up and tell the truth! You say you borrowed it, as you told me. No 'priors,' right?"

"No, ma'am."

"Good. And as your Life Skills teacher, I know you are college-bound. Oh, and show your good grades," I said, printing out his excellent report cards from the past two quarters.

"And?"

"And you tell them you made a mistake and didn't believe your teacher!"

Omar was surprised when I said that he needed to speak up for himself and admit the truth; he was still hoping that if I came with him, his problems would disappear. Next I slapped down his graded and heavily annotated Interactive Student Notebook on the desk in front of him. It was chock-full of teacher comments for perusal. Omar had evidently not taken my concerns seriously.

"Omar, look at this journal entry again!" I advised, pointing to the particular assignment requiring students to chart how much time they spent on select activities, from the time the school day ended until they went to sleep, and then reflect on where they could shave off a few minutes here and there to complete their regular homework and squeeze in a little time for free-choice reading. I remembered feeling totally aghast when I graded the notebooks and discovered that Omar played video games for 7 hours straight every evening. Even worse, the object of his favorite game was stealing cars, and becoming a hero. Even if this was virtual reality, it was glamorizing reckless driving, and living on the edge of a sleazy crime filled life.

Was this an adrenaline rush for the average "good kid"? Well, in this case, this good kid had obviously been brainwashed! I was familiar with the game, since one of my own young teenage boys had brought it home from school in his backpack one day. When I popped it in and saw the array of decadent activities featured, I put it on the couch and plopped down so hard, it broke the DVD! My kids would have no part of a game glorifying crime.

My hunch was correct, a kid could become brainwashed.

My reverie struck pay dirt! "Omar! I've got it! You tell the truth! You tell the judge that you played this game repeatedly for so many hours a day that the fine line between reality and your imaginary world— your 'virtual reality'—was skewed! You brainwashed yourself!"

"That is what happened! Really, Ms. Kurzen!"

"You actually didn't think you were stealing the car; you were just borrowing it, right?"

"Right, I was on the way back. . ."

"When the sirens blared!" I had been sitting here at my desk, correcting papers and thought, *Oh Lord, somebody's brother, or some drug lord is about to get busted!*

"So Ms. Kurzen, about tomorrow?" Omar was relentless, but I firmly stood my ground. I had to lead by example. I told Omar that I respected his opening up to me and sharing his plight. He left knowing that I had full confidence that if he dressed up, showed up, and spoke up with truth and respect for the court, he would most likely be released on probation for a year. I further emphasized that there was a lesson behind the madness that he would have to figure out.

Two days later I was both surprised and humbled that Omar not only showed up in class, but wanted to share his story with the class. Secretly I knew that the school was already abuzz with the Incident of the White

SUV. Omar shared that although he had made many poor choices, the judge was kind and had given him only six months probation for telling the whole truth!

Before he sat down, he turned and gave me a silent thumbs-up!

Mary Anne Kurzen is a National Board-certified teacher with a master's in professional writing. She has over twenty-five years of experience. Her passion for children and lifelong learning has taken her from teaching English, writing, and social studies in secondary schools in large urban school districts in the United States to assisting as a "native speaker" in Germany as well as a small village in rural Nigeria. Kurzen has taught nearly every subject to every grade level, both in the classroom and as a homeschooling parent to her five children, who are all college graduates.

After retiring from full-time teaching, Ms. Kurzen "stepped up her game" by founding Global Educational Training LLC, which offers the ASAP Success and Legacy Writing Programs. Ms. Kurzen's experiential workshops help you get your story out of your head and onto the page, creating your legacy! Ms. Kurzen also writes a column and coaches other writers.

Maryanne@MaryanneKurzen.com

NEVER TOO LATE

Linnaea Mallette

In 1998 my life was aggravated on every front —friendships, marriage, career, and health. I struggled to resist a relapse into substance abuse—thinking it could help manage my mounting despair and depression. It was then I sought the help of a therapist.

After several sessions, the therapist leaned back in her chair, tapped her face thoughtfully, and offered these life-changing words: "Linnaea, I believe that the root of all your problems is your hearing loss."

I resisted at first. "That's ridiculous," I retorted angrily. "I hear *you*!" My therapist asked me to pay closer attention to what I was "hearing." I agreed, but I still could not understand why my hearing would be such a problem. After all, it was merely a simple inconvenience. Wasn't it?

When I began consciously listening to what I was "hearing," I became puzzled. Often speech was unclear—like chunks of sound. Other times I could hear clearly; oftentimes within the course of a single conversation with the same person. What was up with that?

Rather than do what I had always done—pretend that I understood what was said to me—I started to be forthcoming about my hearing loss. I assumed people would know what to do. I found out that they did not.

I discovered myths about hearing loss that even I had succumbed to—myths that got in the way of connection. I started to remember times when, denying my hearing loss, I placed myself in awkward, even dangerous, situations just to be "just like everyone else."

The most foolish activity I participated in was a non-tandem skydiving activity in 1976. I did not anticipate that I wouldn't understand the words from the walkie-talkie strapped to my hip. During the jump, I panicked. I felt myself falling at a speed that seemed too fast, and I couldn't understand if I was being given instruction through the squawk-box.

Thoughts flooded my head: "Should I open my spare parachute or not? I'll look like a fool if I am wrong . . ."

I decided to just hold my breath and take my chances. Obviously I lived. I did not realize it then, but I was willing to *die* than appear foolish because of my hearing loss. That's scary!

One afternoon, while spending an inordinate amount of time trying to decipher a voicemail message, I realized that the most significant challenge I was facing was not my inability to hear well, but my unwillingness to recognize the severity of the loss and its impact on my life. My therapist was right.

At forty-five years old, I decided to support my disability and no longer pretend I didn't have one. The first step was to change my work voicemail recording. I used the outgoing message to instruct callers that I needed to be treated differently: "Please speak clearly and slowly, and especially enunciate numbers. You are leaving a message for a hearing-impaired person." People complied. Some spoke more slowly than others—to a point, it was almost comical. Still, the amount of time, effort, and stress I avoided because I could understand the messages was a real eye-opener. Not only that, I somehow felt like I belonged.

My therapist helped me to see that not understanding conversations and feeling left out was frustrating, tiring, and depressing. Connecting with others is the core of a sense of well-being, of belonging to one's world, of feeling valued. It is the cornerstone of personal and professional success.

I can relate to the words of the remarkable Helen Keller. She wrote: "The problems of deafness are deeper and more complex, if not more important, than those of blindness. Deafness is a much worse misfortune. For it means the loss of the most vital stimulus—the sound of the voice that brings language, sets thoughts astir, and keeps us in the intellectual company of man."

I recalled occasion after occasion where I experienced Ms. Keller's truth. For example, there's the incident of dear, sweet Sonny, an elderly African American gentleman who thought I was a racist because I didn't respond to him when he talked to me as I passed him in the hallway. He copped a real attitude. We had a good laugh when we discovered that what really happened is I did not hear him.

I wondered, "Could it be that all those people who treated me poorly in my life have been thinking, like Sonny, that I didn't like or care for them because I appeared snobby or aloof in my 'not hearing' response?"

Talk about disconnection!

I discovered that the absence of connection is the biggest tragedy of hearing loss. Not only for those with a hearing loss, but also for all those near to them—whether a family member, friend, customer, client, employer, or employee.

Over the course of the following years, I studied how communication is actually accomplished. I discovered why my hearing could fluctuate so dramatically during the course of a single conversation. I devised simple yet helpful ways to connect, despite hearing loss. I felt compelled to share my insights with others. I started blogging.

I blogged about the common myths surrounding hearing loss; how to recognize hearing loss; the realistic expectations of hearing aids; the benefits and detriments of hearing loss as one moves about one's daily life. I created a simple technique comprised of three components, encapsulated in the acronym "CPR," to keep a conversation from dying.

I wrote not from an academic, "schooled" point of view, although I did draw upon some of those resources, but as a person who struggled with this physical disability since birth. Honest. Up front. No holds barred. I felt the posts had to be that way to be truly helpful.

Those posts helped me to compile books about my experiences and discoveries. One even became an Amazon best seller. I began receiving invitations to talk about hearing loss to all kinds of organizations. I love seeing the light of understanding shine from my audience's eyes. Afterwards many comment, "Wow, I always thought shouting helps!" (It doesn't.)

I had the privilege of sharing my insights and strategies globally as a TEDx speaker. Someone remarked to me, "Linnaea, I believe what you shared will impact the way the world communicates."

Today I marvel at how far I have come since sitting in that therapist's chair. Her words still sound loudly in my heart, and I am appreciative of that wisdom. Hearing now, with a new understanding, gives me the opportunity to help others worldwide to keep the connection alive.

Linnaea Mallete is a professional speaker and author of three books, Hearing Loss Tips, Hearing Loss CPR, *and her latest book on overcoming adversity titled* Thirty Tips to Get Out of the Pits. *In 2013 she took an early retirement from a thirty-three-year career at UCLA in Research Administration. During her tenure she served as a training coordinator and was nominated for the Chancellor's True Blue Award for her endeavors. She is passionate about photography, quotes, and graphic art, which she employs to design T-shirts. She resides in Los Angeles with her husband of thirty years, Bruce Mallette, a classical violinist.*

www.LinnaeaMallette.com

BEYOND MY WILDEST DREAMS

Sue Mandell

Here's the picture: I'm twenty-nine years old, I live in a Navy town, I work in a bar, and drugs and alcohol have taken over my life.

I would like to tell you that it wasn't my fault, that I lived the way I did because my parents beat me. But I can't say that because it would be a lie. I had an amazing childhood! I participated in family decisions, and my parents always told me how much they loved me and how proud they were of me. I never for a moment doubted my place in the family.

The reason I lived the way I did was because I had crossed that invisible line, going from having fun to This Is My Life.

Fast-forward two years: I'm at a friend's house, and her husband comes downstairs at 6:00 a.m. There we sit, at her kitchen counter. We had stayed up all night partying *again*. That was the first time I'd ever felt shame and remorse and, though I will never know what prompted me, for the first time I said, "I have a problem, and I don't know what to do about it."

I had no idea how my life would change forever as I said those words out loud.

I had been existing in the shadows of my life for a very long time. I didn't know who I was or what I wanted. I only knew that I was pretending. I spent every waking moment doing drugs, looking for drugs, or telling lies about why I was late or was unable to keep my commitments. I am 5'8" tall and weighed 123 pounds. I had gone from a high school graduate with a great future to someone who had dropped out of four colleges and universities.

I did the hardest thing I've ever had to do: I called my mom. I told her I had a problem, didn't know where to turn, and asked her for help. I started seeing a counselor who pulled no punches. He set me on the path to recovery, and I really believe he saved my life.

The miracle happened: I stayed sober an entire day, then two days, and then three days. I hadn't been without "something" in my system for many years. As I continued to work with him, he asked the hard questions and wouldn't accept the crap I could pass off on everyone else.

I had finished my inventory in Alcoholics Anonymous, that infamous fourth step. I was excited because I would *never have to go back to the hell I'd left*. He helped me to admit that I'm not immune or invincible and that I'm only one drink away from losing everything. He asked me what one thing would make me slip over the side of this lifeboat I was on, back into the icy waters of using—and death.

I told him I would be most vulnerable if something happened to one of my parents. He had me make a plan: what I would do if something happened to them. That day in his office I made the plan that saved my life.

When I got *that* call, I didn't have to think. I called my sponsor, reached out to Alcoholics Anonymous in the city my mom lived in, and shared my fears and feelings in meetings. The decisions were already made. I didn't have to wonder what to do or worry about staying sober. I had the plan, and the plan kicked in, as if by magic. Instead of getting loaded like I did when my dad had his first stroke, rendering me unable to even make it to the hospital, I was there for both my mom and dad when they needed me.

I never want to give the impression that just because I got clean and sober, my life became idyllic. Anyone who tells you that is lying. With my mentor's coaching, I came to realize that I got sober to get back out there into the world to *live life*, not to die horribly in a dark corner.

After we lost my mom, I helped my dad move closer when he was ready. I was blessed to spend several more years with him as both his daughter and friend. On my dad's last day with us, my brother and I sat on either side of his bed holding his hands. We watched the last game of the World Series with him as he passed from this world. People like me, a drunk and an addict, don't usually get to be present for those precious moments in life; we're too immersed in our disease.

There have been lots of ups and downs in my thirty years of sobriety. I've been married and divorced, I've lost both of my amazing parents, and my home was destroyed in a fire. I've graduated college with not only my bachelor's degree, but my master's degree too. I've had two amazing careers.

I came home from work one day to a note from my husband saying he'd taken my five dogs and wasn't coming back. I tell you these things not because they are extraordinary and not because I'm special, but because they are *life*, and I lived them sober.

I've had a life beyond anything I could ever have imagined when I first asked for help. But I haven't told you the best part yet: my brother, whom

I could barely tolerate and who could barely tolerate me, is now my best friend. I can't imagine my life if he weren't in it.

Today my joy and passion in life is to help others as I've been helped. I would be honored to help you or a loved one to go from "merely existing" to "living a life beyond your wildest dreams."

Through her company, Better Me Solutions, Sue Mandell helps sober people in recovery learn to live their dreams by helping them transition from merely existing to empowerment. In recovery since June 10, 1988, Sue is an author, speaker, trainer, NLP Master Practitioner, Master Life Coach, Master Executive Coach, and a Master Timeline Dynamics Practitioner.

SueMandell@BetterMeSolutions.com

ENERGY, PEOPLE, AND PETS

Sue Marting

As with most of us, our life's mission seems to evolve over time. My mission came into clearer focus when I was diagnosed with a health condition for which traditional medicine had no cure. I'm a searcher so rather than give up, I decided to find another way. I got my inspiration from my work with animals. I had been working with animals, doing massage with them, and I knew the health benefits they received, so I educated myself on some less traditional practices as I sought treatment for myself. Reiki was the first modality I studied; it made perfect sense to me. The body is made up of energy, and Reiki is a practice that balances the energy in the body, allowing the body to function at its optimal level of health. When the body is functioning at its own optimum level, it can heal itself, just as it does on a daily basis. I have used Reiki and other modalities in my own healing, and it has become a daily practice for me. What I love about energy work is that it is a complete approach that focuses on body, mind, and soul.

Working with People

I wanted to share my newfound "magical experience" with others. Many of my clients have stress-induced illnesses, physical pain, or emotional trauma (mostly from childhood), and through energy work we have been able to reduce stress, release tension, and increase relaxation, allowing the body to use its own ability to regenerate and heal itself. It is truly amazing that when we can quiet the mind and just let our body do what it was designed to do, miracles happen. I have had clients who have come in with back pain, and after a session of balancing and relaxation, the pain went away. Our body is designed to be in a state of balance; unfortunately everyday life tends to throw us out of balance.

I work with a nonprofit organization, and we have worked with veterans with Post Traumatic Stress Syndrome (PTSD). Reiki has been very helpful in aiding veterans with PTSD and insomnia feel less anxious and overwhelmed. Some of the results have been truly transformative.

Working with Pets

Animals are very sensitive to energy and emotion. They are sensitive to their caretaker's energy, the energy at the vet's office, and the energy of guests in your home. How many times have you had a guest that your dog just did not like? Because animals are so sensitive to energy, they are perfect for energy work. One of the cats I am most fond of remembering is a cat named Grey Guy. He was diagnosed with FIP (feline infectious peritonitis), but through energy work and using different modalities of healing, Grey Guy was able to live longer (with a good quality of life) than any other cat with FIP my vet was aware of.

When you listen to animals, they will show you the way. They will let you know what they like and don't like. Generally they enjoy massage and energy work. It can help with pain management and healing, providing a very soothing environment for them. One of the purposes of energy work is to raise the vibration for you, your pet, and the environment. You might find that if you meditate at home, your pet may curl up and just want to lie by you; this is because of the soothing energy that is surrounding you.

How Pets Are Helping People

People have pets in their lives for many reasons. They provide companionship, give their owners the opportunity to exercise, reduce stress, provide protection, expose their owners to new interests and activities, and provide daily routine and structure. Our pets provide great health benefits for us as well. Just petting our dog or cat reduces stress, lowers blood pressure, lessens anxiety, and provides a calming atmosphere for us. For many years therapy dogs have been used to help people of all ages with disabilities. Today it is very common for emotional support animals, comfort animals, and therapy dogs to be in hospitals or assisted living homes to provide healing to the patients.

People understand the benefits that pets provide to them, but they are sometimes surprised when they start working with me to find out other benefits that they were not aware of. Pets have the ability absorb people's negative energy, process it, and let it go. That is one way they serve us. Have you ever noticed that if you are sick, your pet will keep you company? I had a client that had a cut and bruised leg and faithfully every night his cat, McKinley, would lie right by the injured leg. Animals have intuition, and they pick up so much information that most of us are not even aware of. Some people are afraid of dogs, for example, and who is usually the first person a dog will run up to in a crowd? It's usually the person who is afraid of the dog.

Since pets are so sensitive to our energy, to take the best care of yourself and your pets, de-stress before you come into the house and pet your animals; otherwise they will pick up on your bad day. They are also very sensitive to tones, so don't yell unless there is an emergency. If your pet gets sick, ask yourself, "Is this a sign for me? Is there something I need to know or watch out for? Keep your mind and heart open to your pet. You might be surprised what you learn.

Sue Marting is a gifted natural wellness expert with an emphasis on healing the human body and animals with six different modalities of energy. She has transformed personal experiences and classroom and experiential learnings into her passion and calling as a teacher, energy healer, and intuitive. Sue is a Reiki Master Teacher/Practitioner, #1 Internationally Best Selling Author, professional speaker, and tapping instructor. She is certified in sound healing and is also trained in other balancing techniques to provide a holistic approach to health and life. Sue obtained her MBA from Xavier University. Her greatest privilege, however, is being Bill's mom.

www.TotalEnergyHealth.com

NOT ONLY SURVIVING, BUT THRIVING

Carey McLean

I could never have imagined what it feels like to be told that you are about to start the fight of your life, and cancer is the opponent. After hearing those three words from my breast surgeon on the phone, "They found cancer," my life changed forever, as well as the lives of the people around me. My hope is that my story impacts others and encourages them to be their best self and to always fight a good fight. You never know when you're going to need it.

On December 20, 2014, I was excited as ever to be going home to Minnesota for a two-week holiday visit. I took a red-eye from Sacramento that was to land in Minneapolis at 5:30 a.m. After I landed, I went to the nearest Orangetheory Fitness Studio in Apple Valley to make my 8:15 a.m. workout, as an OTFer groupie would.

Later that day, I had a conversation with my Aunt Deb that would change my life forever. I owe my life, and this year's outcome, to her for that one little conversation. And I can never thank my family and friends enough for all their support and love that I received this year. I do believe that things happen for a reason, no matter how good or bad we perceive them to be.

While I was home, I told my mom, "I think I found something." It felt like a mini golf ball in my right breast, and I could move it a little by grabbing onto it with my thumb and index finger.

Every day, for two weeks, I knew it was there, kept checking it…but planned on it being nothing. I made a decision right then that I would not spend energy on something that I could not control. The only thing I could control was how I lived my life going forward.

Immediately after returning home to Sacramento, I saw my family doctor. That led to a mammogram and ultrasound. Doctors told me that it was probably benign because the tumor did not seem to have the characteristics of cancer. Either way, the lump was bothering me, and I wanted it removed.

I was referred to a breast surgeon to help me through this journey. My first surgery date was set for January 28. The fine needle aspiration before surgery did not indicate cancer either, so my doctor proceeded to take out the tumor.

In January 2014, I was blessed to be able to attend Maryann Ehmann's "Create Your Magnificent Life" at Coronado Beach. After going to this amazing three-day event, my goal for 2014 was to talk with God on a regular basis and journal what I heard. This became something that I would do in order to gain clarity and guidance in my life.

About two days before my first scheduled surgery, I wrote the following journal entry:

Monday, January 26, 2015
Dear God,
Why am I so strong and able to handle this? (As I am driving to work, crying)

Dear Carey,
Because I made you that way.

After I heard those words in my head, my tears immediately stopped. I felt a kind of peace that couldn't be ignored. I knew I was going to be okay. With every decision I made in 2015, I waited for that same feeling and accepted it. My only job was to research, evaluate, make a decision, and move on. Very similar to what I do in business.

The morning of the lumpectomy, which would tell me if it was cancerous or not, I made the following journal entry:

Wednesday, January 28, 2015
Dear God,
Why am I able to get through this surgery and move on with my everyday life as if it was just a bump in the road?

Dear Carey,
It is just a bump... A little one at that :). You will recover amazingly fast and be back golfing, working out, and enjoying life in no time!

After surgery, I was led to believe that the lump was removed and that it was benign. My doctor told me the following: Fibroadenoma of the breast is a benign tumor. Benign tumor means it is not caused by cancer.

I thought I was in the clear and was so grateful that it was benign and would not affect me further. About a week later, I got a phone call while sitting in the San Diego airport on my way to Baltimore for a software developer event. As I talked to my doctor on the phone, I heard him say, "They found cancer." Tears rolled down my face immediately as I sat in the waiting area to board my flight.

I made the following journal after I got the news:

Thursday, February 5, 2015
Dear God,
Why am I strong enough and courageous enough to make it through this?

Dear Carey,
Because I made you that way and you never back down from a challenge. There's some connected reason why you are taking this path. Find it and meet it with the strength and courage I have gifted you with and that you use so well. You have so many people that love you and support you every step of the way. Utilize their positive energy as you often do.

On February 5, 2015, at age 38, I was diagnosed with breast cancer. I made a decision early on that I would not change events on my calendar if I could help it. This included my business and golf events that I loved so much. Eight weeks after my bilateral mastectomy on my birthday, I won my Chapter Championship and advanced to semi-finals.

On August 1, eleven days after my third chemo treatment, I won semi-finals and advanced to finals. I played both days at the EWGA finals in Palm Springs, California, ten weeks after my final chemo treatment. I didn't win, but I had a blast, and I got to show up. Surviving. And thriving.

Carey McLean is The App Chicks' creator, technical guru, and designer. Carey is goal-oriented, the queen of troubleshooting, and repeatedly gets the job done in the most efficient manner. As the App Chicks' CEO, her cutting-edge skills transform her customers' ideas into reality. It is her acute intuition and swift implementation that sets Carey apart from the rest.

www.TheAppChicks.com

WASHING OFF THE MUCK
AND DARING TO DREAM

Joanne Neweduk

After a major life event rocked me to my core and sent all I held dear into question, I moved through life in a strange, fog-like state for a while, feeling overwhelmed and weighed down by the muck of life. At the time it felt as if my worst fears had come true. In retrospect I now see it as a blessing and the catalyst to truly living a life that "rocks."

I was a full-time, stay-at-home mother of three active children; a supportive daughter to an aging, ailing mother; a soon to be ex-wife; a committed volunteer in many capacities; and the list goes on. Although I loved what I was doing, I did not always act from a stance of power and choice. I felt overly responsible for everyone else's health and happiness and had lost sight of my own. My life revolved around helping everyone else fulfill their dreams. Yet no one asked me what my dreams were, least of all myself. Perhaps it's because I had forgotten to dream.

Bit by bit, through a sequence of events, friendships, workshops, and amazing opportunities, I learned to wash off the muck of life that was weighing me down and hiding my joy. I shed fear, sadness, aloneness, hurt, embarrassment, the "supermom" syndrome, and the "I must be strong for everyone else" syndrome. I learned to recognize that I had constructed a strength that was both brittle and fragile. Learning to be vulnerable and trusting that I would be supported was the magic that transformed my life. I embraced the innate, inner strength, and brilliant light that I possess and allowed it to be flexible, subtle, and yes, vulnerable at times.

One story I recall occurred when I was invited with a group of other people to attend a sweat lodge. I desperately wanted to be part of this incredible opportunity, but I feared that I might not be able to handle the experience due to a health issue. I was worried that I might spoil the event for the others. My old self simply would have declined and missed out on the opportunity. Instead I plucked up my courage to speak to the organizer (the woman who would be doing the pour) and shared my fears. She looked at me with compassion and, in a matter of fact way, touched my arm and declared, "Well, if you don't feel well, we'll simple take care of you. You'll sit by me just in case." I felt a well of emotion bubble up inside of me. I knew I would be safe and indeed, that evening was one of the most unique and incredible experiences I have ever had. That night I had the humbling opportunity to be the receiver of care and love, and it transformed me. A layer of muck had been washed away.

Today I am so very grateful for experiences like this, because I frequently work with people who struggle with self-care or accepting support. This has fostered my ability to create a safe space for the strong to be vulnerable—an ability that has come in handy with all my roles both personally and professionally.

Over the years I have been willing to say yes to incredible opportunities. Bit by bit I have dared to dream, and now I truly delight in supporting others to do the same.

To be a Woman Who Rocks holds a different meaning for each of us. For me it means:

...knowing happiness as my most comfortable state of being.

...daring to step through fear and out of my comfort zone to endlessly create anew.

...having the courage to return to school and reclaim my RN status, a challenging, two-year journey filled with incredible rewards. I increased my confidence, I renewed my love of learning, and I was blessed with the support of family and friends cheering me on.

...opening my heart to co-create a relationship built on mutual love, respect, and support. I cherish it beyond measure, and I love that it's filled with fun, adventure, and "wink wink."

...transforming my life by embracing gratitude on a daily basis and recently acting on a dream to create and publish a gratitude journal.

...feeling my heart filled with joy as I watch my children grow into amazing, unique individuals, knowing I've had a part in their growth as they have in mine.

...daring to step into the world of entrepreneurship and learning how to run a business or two.

...becoming an author, coach, and facilitator.

...training in Light Therapy, Sound Wellness, and Belief Repatterning.

...leading Fabulous@50 Calgary, an organization that celebrates women in midlife.

…founding Brilliant Light Wellness: Shedding Light on Health, Love, and Happiness.

…learning to generously give and graciously receive.

…dreaming and not holding back on my dreams.

Life gets mucky at times. We get splashed, sometimes even fully submerged. It's our responsibility to wash that muck off on a regular basis. We do not need to stay covered in the muck of our hurts and sorrows. We get to choose whether allow it to weigh us down and hide our joy or use it to scrub ourselves fresh, making us healthier and more radiant. We can shine our most brilliant light in health, love, and happiness. We can be Women Who Rock!

Joanne Neweduk is an oncology nurse, author, coach, and facilitator. She is the founder of Brilliant Light Wellness and runs Fabulous@50 Calgary. Joanne teaches explorations on gratitude, generosity, and celebration. She frequently contributes to the Be Fabulous *e-magazine and is a co-author of the award winning books* Frock Off: Living Undisguised *and* Fabulous@50 The Re-Experience. *Joanne has a decades-long involvement with volunteerism and event planning, and she is the past president of a humanitarian charity, Medical Mercy Canada.*

www.BrilliantLightWellness.com

LIVE HEALTHY. LIVE HAPPY.

Dr. Aurora Ongaro

2:26am, youngest is crying, bad dream. Cuddle her back to sleep, crawl back into bed. 3:32am, four-year-old climbs into our bed. Wake up with alarm at 6:15am, husband is already up. I extract myself from the small limbs wrapped around my neck and sneak into the shower. A quick kiss good-bye from the hubby at 6:30am when he leaves for school. Dress sleepy girls, carry them both out to the car, and get them to our dayhome. Eat a homemade granola breakfast bar in car.

8:00am, I'm at the office sipping an almond milk latte, analyzing the chriopractic X-rays for the day and catching up on paperwork. I start with patients at 9:00am, and we hit the ground running. I have two new patients and twenty-four checkups scheduled today. A newer patient is excited that the recurrent low back and hip pain he's had for the last three years is gone. Another tells me she no longer has daily headaches and that I've changed her life. I'm thrilled for them and grateful that with NUCCA chiropractic care I can help people feel so much better. Another patient tells me that she's noticed that I always have a smile on my face; she asks me, "How is it that you're always so happy?"

I finish up with patients at 3:30pm, then catch up on emails and the lesson prep for my dance business. I'm teaching advanced level dance tomorrow night, and the choreography needs tweaking.

4:15pm, I hit the gym; I'm in and out in under thirty minutes. I pick the kids up and get home for supper (thank God my husband knows his way around the kitchen). The rest of the evening is family time, then food prep after the girls are in bed and quality time with hubby. My story deadline is looming, but *Game of Thrones* is calling us. No contest there. Bedtime is 10:00pm.

This is my day, four days a week. It's at once hectic and rewarding. At times it's borderline overwhelming. And I love it!

From an outside perspective, it might look insane, but it inspires me.

It's a healthy life; beautiful and balanced by the three days a week I'm home with my family and careful attention to my mental, physical, and emotional needs.

Lots of women face hectic lives. It's likely you do too. Between work, family obligations, personal interests, and other demands on our time, many of us feel stretched to the limit. But balance is possible—I've found mine, and I know you can find yours. The golden question is *how*?

You need to take care of you.

Exactly what that means differs from person to person. There is no magic formula. But there are five key aspects I live by and continue to work on.

1. Engage in something you're interested in and passionate about. My passion for health and wellness started when I was fifteen and underwent a treatment that completely changed my and my family's life. I'm fortunate that my passion aligns with my career choice to be a NUCCA chiropractor. The desire to help people and be healthy continues to influence both my lifelong learning and my daily decisions. Whatever *your* passion may be, work it into your life. It doesn't need to be your career, but it will give your days purpose and fire.

2. Take care of your body. No excuses! It's difficult to love life if you are in pain. If you're hurting, search for treatments and experts to help you and guide you toward better health. The doctors in my office maintain my spinal alignment as it is fundamental to my well-being. My naturopath provided simple changes that greatly improved my immune system. My massage therapist works out tight muscles and relieves stress.

3. You gotta move! It's necessary for your body, and it improves your mood. You have the time—and if you feel like you don't, make it. Take thirty minutes a day, five to six days a week, to put your health on the top of your "to-do" list. My kids know they only get a cartoon at home if I'm on the treadmill. Don't like running? Pick something you do like. One of my favorite movements is dance. Dance is exercise disguised as fun, and I have fun weekly! To keep my body to be strong now and years from now, I also mix in weight training and set clear goals to keep me motivated. Literally and figuratively, I aim to be a strong role model for my patients and my daughters.

4. Fuel yourself well. Recently our family has put an increased focus on nutrition. When you start educating yourself, it becomes shocking how food choices can impact your health. While I won't list all the conferences attended, books read, and documentaries watched, there are consistent messages that we have taken to heart and are implementing in our home.

We've rebalanced our plates; at least 90 percent of our meals are plant-based now. Most of our meals are cooked from scratch. It takes more time, but it's time we spend as a family.

5. Seek out and accept help. Overwhelmed? It's OK to ask for help. This was a difficult lesson for me to learn. Professional athletes have coaches and a support team, and supermoms need them too. Over the years, I've worked with a professional coach, worked with mentors, attended personal development conferences, and read books. I call on friends or family if I need some downtime or help with keeping my ducks in a row. I have endless gratitude for all the help and support I've received.

There's a trap we sometimes fall into: we think we *need* to do it all. You don't. Sometimes things will come up that will throw your balance off. That's OK. Accept it and rebalance as soon as you can. It's about progress, not perfection. Figure that out, and you'll wake each morning excited to start the day.

I do.

Dr. Aurora Ongaro is a clinical practitioner at NUCCA Chiropractic. For over thirteen years she has helped thousands of people gain better health in multiple areas of their lives. As an award-winning dancer, nutrition enthusiast, and mother of two, Dr. Ongaro understands the importance of a balanced approach to health and well-being. In addition to managing a busy clinical practice, Dr. Ongaro owns and operates Move Studios and has competed in her first obstacle race. This year she will be featured in the documentary On a Scale of 1 to 10, *a film exploring treatment for chronic pain.*

www.symmetryspinalcare.com

WELCOME TO FINISHING SCHOOL

Roberta Perry

"Welcome to Finishing School" . . . which is really the end of the story, so let's start at the beginning. All good stories have a start, and this is mine.

It happened that on a cloudy Seattle day the "steaks were high" (pun) when I got my foot in the door at Stuart Anderson's Steak Restaurants. My goal was some lofty rung on the corporate ladder, and I had high hopes. Months later, as a secretary for the entertainment director, I was getting nowhere. Where was the first rung and how was I going to climb it? Meanwhile I was being schooled, in a more or less humorous way, by some of my female coworkers. "You can't wear nylons with support toes." "No slacks in the office for us women." "Where did you get that mini-skirt outfit?"

I wish I could say that a lightbulb went off, but in fact I was finally embarrassed enough to enroll in a nine-week John Robert Powers Modeling Agency etiquette class for businesswomen. Every week for nine weeks, I had to wear a different outfit from my closet to show my style. And every week I flunked and had to walk the proverbial plank in front of the others. It was like failing recess. Did I even have a personal style?

What I desperately needed was a mentor, and during week nine, I found one. Sheila was our hairstylist consultant. She said, "Get $500 together—we're going shopping." It was the shopping trip that changed my *future*. I went into the dressing room looking like a college grad wannabe and walked out looking every bit the executive. An exquisitely tailored navy-blue suit, two blouses, pumps, and a London Fog raincoat. To my surprise, the outfit was commanding, not stuffy. Following John T. Malloy's advice in his bestselling book *Dress for Success*, I decided then and there *to dress as though I already had the job*. Then I started watching not only my boss but my boss' boss—his clothes, his attitude when he walked into a room, his gestures and deportment, his general personal presentation. And from that I awoke to a broader awareness. It all boiled down to one word:

impact. He was creating an impact without saying a thing, opening a door to eventual success before the first word was spoken.

By now I was on the right track. There was so much more behind success in business than a "de facto dress code."

In time I worked out two simple rules that enable the chance of success when dealing with people in any business setting:

1. If you're presenting to Coca Cola, don't go in wearing Pepsi "blue and red."

2. Act like you mean it—and mean it!

Naturally, the key to my own success along this line was working out—at the detail level —my own presentation in any and all types of business relations (and may I point out here that you can remove the word *business* from this sentence and expand your success in all areas of life).

What was the image I wanted to communicate visually as well as verbally? What did I want to project in that critical three seconds after I entered a room or shook a hand or smiled hello to someone? Was I nervous or feeling pressured? Was I asking in my style and manner for a license to survive? Or was I creating the impact that would generate the exact response I wanted? I listed dozens of scenarios and created appropriate personal presentation factors for each one. I started defining the exact impact I wanted to make in business situations and then owning the level of personal commitment and action necessary to achieve that impact. It's a process that continues to this day.

If you get the two rules above dialed in and fine-tuned for yourself, what is possible? For me it was the "ten-minute, multimillion-dollar deal." Early in the 2000s I was working with an international entertainment investment company based in Los Angeles. A Tennessee client wanted to discuss particulars and arranged to fly us to their offices for a meeting. On the scheduled day we got together promptly at 9:00 a.m., and within ten minutes they had agreed to the terms previously outlined and we immediately signed a letter of intent. Later in the evening we were all having dinner, and I asked the female senior executive how she had come to the decision so readily. I will never forget her response: "It was easy. You walked in wearing a Chanel suit and Ferragamo shoes and carrying a Gucci briefcase. And your partner was dressed in the same high-end style. Both of you had a positive air of success! I knew then you were successful and exactly what we wanted."

A great philosopher once said that life is art. Some women are born works of art with style and grace. Not me. I had to learn to pick up a brush and paint my own way to Tiffany's and diamond stud earrings. So take a minute here for yourself. Try this little drill. On a piece of paper, describe your own personal presentation. Does it say executive? Or temp worker? What is your attitude? Does it create an effect even before you say anything? And make sure it creates the appropriate impact; you *could* wear jeans with shredded knees, but is that for a barbecue fest or the boardroom?

Have a good time with this . . . and "Welcome to Finishing School"!

Roberta Perry is the senior vice-president of Edwards Technologies, Inc., and president of Roberta Perry & Associates. She has served as chairman of the Nightclub and Bar Association; was president of the Themed Entertainment Association; sat on the Seattle Fair Campaign and Practices Commission; has been the international board director for Toastmasters International; and currently serves on the board for Lawrence Anthony's Earth Organization.

www.edwardstechnologies.com

GIVE IT YOUR ALL

Luz Sanchez

I learned to read and write when I was three years old. I owe my first experience with words, numbers, and drawings to the woman who gave life to me, my mother. She only reached the second grade of elementary school because she had to work in the tomato fields in a small town in Mexico. I appreciate her effort and endurance.

The first few years of my education flew by so fast. From kindergarten, my teachers promoted me ahead to the second grade, and everything was fine until that point. In the following years I struggled to keep up with my school assignments and homework because my siblings and I had to work: trimming the loose threads of clothing, washing clothes, and shelling thousands of seeds and nuts. My mother held down several jobs and often left me home alone to care for my siblings. Unfortunately my father was an alcoholic and our home life was dominated by domestic violence; he destroyed everything we tried so hard to build.

When I turned eight, my father wanted me to stop studying so I could work full time. Huge fights ensued, and for days after I was afraid to go to school because I thought I would come home to find my mother dead. I worried about my mom and prayed constantly to a saint who I believed would protect us. When my mom enrolled me in middle school, my father beat her up so badly that she spent days in the hospital. She still encouraged me to continue moving forward. She would tell me, "*Tu hechale ganas.*" This translates roughly into "Give it your all" or "Do it with all your might."

I wanted to continue studying and growing despite all the obstacles, but sometimes those obstacles were outside my personal control. We barely made enough money from our work to survive, so there was not enough to buy school supplies. Sometimes there was not enough money to ride the bus or to buy shoes. We each had one pair of shoes, and my mom extended the lives of our shoes by buying oversized shoes that had room for us to grow into them. When our feet outgrew the shoes, she would cut off the front so our little toes wouldn't get hurt. She also made our clothes from pieces of discarded fabric from the factories near our house.

Living at home was like living in an inferno. Thankfully my curiosity propelled me to explore everything I saw around me. When I got a job washing dishes in a woman's house, I found the book called *A Thousand and One Nights*. This book changed my life. It provided wisdom and allowed me to use my imagination to escape to different worlds from the conditions I was living in. The protagonist was a woman with great power in the art of storytelling. When my father saw me reading, he would scream at me to stop wasting my time and tell me go wash the dishes. I would do all the work I had to do with a huge desire in my heart to again hold the book in my hands, absorbing page after page.

When I attended junior high school, our teacher took us to several museums. I fell in love with archaeology, anthropology, and art. I became very proud of my pre-Columbian ancestry, my heritage and roots, and all that my ancestors left us. This motivated me to continue learning.

I lived in two different worlds: the outside world where I had to be strong and resilient to survive all the adversities of life, and the world of my imagination where I could lose myself. The inner, imaginary world was where I wanted to live.

I truly felt that I didn't fit in my family or society; I wanted to study and become somebody, but I often heard my father and uncles say that education was not for women. According to the men around me, we should be their servants, take care of our houses, and have children. What I saw is that most of the women around me were the foundation of the Mexican society. They were not only housewives; they were also the breadwinners, the fathers, the anchors. Yet in spite of all of that, we were subjected to abuse and the idea that we amounted to nothing.

The obstacles to getting an education grew when I wanted to enroll in high school. In Mexico City, high schools are overpopulated and as a result extremely selective regarding admissions. Miraculously I was accepted and kept moving forward in spite of all the storms around me. At the conclusion of high school, I attended an international film festival. The movies I saw were something I had never experienced in my life. The festival expanded the horizons of my life to include countless possibilities. I knew I wanted to make films, but endless searching failed to turn up opportunities.

It was not until a decade later, after immigrating to the United States and struggling with numerous challenges, that I realized I could do it.

I was a single mother without a job, without any friends, and I did not speak English. I had to start from the very bottom, but I kept my faith strong. My son was one of my motivations. I wanted a better life for us, and now, living in this country, I had the opportunity. So I gave it my all. I worked and studied tirelessly day and night for years. I started with ESL (English as a Second Language) classes and kept going until I received my four-year university degree. Looking back, I can see that serendipitously I have always been divinely guided and supported.

Even when you encounter obstacles in your path, stick to your vision, the vision that God has given you. Do not let other people control your life. Know that you have the power to get away from the people who drain you, make you sick, and suck the life out of you. Know that even when it feels like you are in the middle of darkness, you are the light and you are divinely guided and supported. Do not let the appearances of the moment cloud your vision. Keep your faith strong, keep moving forward, and keep the fire burning within yourself. Know that you can accomplish anything in life and *give it your all.*

Luz Sanchez immigrated to the United States from a small, impoverished town near Mexico City at age twenty-six with her four-year-old son. With a dream of pursuing a career in film, Luz was determined to become fluent in English as quickly as possible. While juggling several jobs and caring for her son, she enrolled in English immersion classes at the community college. She later transferred to Cal State Northridge, where she earned a degree in cinema and TV arts. Today Luz is a video editor, speaker, and mother of two children who never lost sight of a brighter future.

REFLECTIONS OF A BESTSELLING AUTHOR

Merle M. Singer

Here I am included in a book about successful women. How can that be? What makes me successful? What have I done? The first thing that comes to mind is all the things I haven't done yet. And then I think of all the women I've taught and coached, and pretty much everybody I know, regardless of their level of accomplishment. Most people I know are similar to me. They are impressed with everyone else's accomplishments and darn near oblivious to their own successes.

We are warned not to be too prideful, but most people I know are too humble. The problem with being too humble is that you don't value your own abilities enough. You then don't feel worthy and capable to make the effort to take your work to a bigger stage. I too struggle with using modesty as an excuse for not reaching higher instead of using humility simply as a spiritual value.

So let me forge the way for all women and men of the world in taking ownership of our accomplishments. Of course my first great accomplishment was being born. I was eager to be born, and I announced my intentions declaratively. My mother assured me I wasted no time in entering the world. My second accomplishment was surviving childhood. There was talk of infantile paralysis with lots of accompanying doctor visits. Then there was my mother's merciless teasing. She was much meaner than she realized, and it took a lot of patience to hang around at home long enough to get my college degree in teaching so I could support myself. I went on to get my master's in education as well.

Actually my mother's teasing was the stimulus for learning how to read facial expressions and deal with my mom and other personalities. I didn't realize it at the time, but it was the basis for my current adult career as the Relationship Miracle Worker. I knew I had talent in that area when as a teen, I gave my mother marital advice—and she listened—and it worked. I bet each of you reading this have your own version of childhood that took courage on your part, and here you are today, a proof of your earlier success.

Other successes: I joined Toastmasters and achieved their highest designation, Distinguished Toastmaster. I was president of my temple, Beth Shir Shalom, when they merged from two congregations into one and needed an objective set of eyes with a clear focus on creating a unified family. I was civilian chair of the Hollywood Community Police Advisory Board. I've received numerous awards, including Woman of the Year from the Hollywood Chamber of Commerce. I even did a comedy skit at the Hollywood Improv (https://www.youtube.com/watch?v=amaNqZe4zJ0).

My longest standing success is my marriage of fifty years. That's pretty incredible! In fact my husband, Nathan, and I amaze ourselves with our accomplishment at least once a week. What's amazing about it is that Nathan came with two kids (Ruthie, fourteen, and Joseph, nine). We added Isaac to the crew and made it all work; it took the both of us. And wonderfully there are now spouses and grandchildren that have joined the troupe.

But once there was trouble in paradise. In year nineteen we were close to divorcing. Even couples therapy didn't help—well, it helped, but not enough. That's when I decided to take a different approach. Instead of trying to make the marriage better, I put that to the side and concentrated on simply making myself happy. Doing what I wanted to do and checking things off my personal bucket list. I just wanted to feel relevant and on-purpose, whether I was married or not. It worked.

What was so interesting about concentrating on doing things that brought me joy was the unintended consequences. I was now happy. Now my default response was to laugh and find humor. I treated everyone in my life with a sparkle in my eye, including my husband. He was astounded, and he responded very positively. It didn't change him, but it changed how he acted, because I changed the environment. This is an interesting phenomenon.

The things I learned in that journey followed universal truths, so that anyone doing their version of the same thing can get the same happy results. That's when I created the 3 Steps to Transform Your Relationship Experience course. It's such a great course that I'm currently making even better by revising and updating it.

In the meantime, I just published my first best seller on Amazon. It's called *Cracking the Relationship Code: The Key to Happy Relationships at Home and at Work*. All those smaller successes along the way have led me here. Finally I feel like a Rock Star.

Let me finish with a quote from an ancient scholar, Hillel:

If I am not for myself, who will be for me?
If I am only for myself, what am I?
If not now, when?

Merle M. Singer is a bestselling author, speaker, and coach. As a Relationship Miracle Worker, Merle works with you to pinpoint your pain quickly and then reveals effective techniques that dissolve your relationship misery—all this, without your partner/colleague (or anyone else) knowing.Check out her website and get a free gift.

www.relationshipmiracleworker.com/freegift

LIFE TRANSITIONS

Karen Strauss

How did a love of reading turn into a passion for publishing?

My father used to read to me all the time when I was a little girl. My favorite book was *Auntie Katushka and the Poppyseed Cakes*. I remember laughing and laughing even when my father just mentioned the title. Throughout the years we read hundreds of books—from Dr Seuss to Maurice Sendak to Shakespeare.

My love of literature continued throughout high school and college. I was an English major, and I remember having arguments with my teachers about my interpretation of some of Shakespeare's passages in some of his plays. This was fun for me. I thought I wanted to be an English and drama teacher, but I really hated the beauracracy . . . too stodgy and too many rules for me to follow. Anyone who knows me knows I hate to follow rules; I've always wanted to march to the beat of a different drummer. I did not yet know that this very quality is a major asset if you want to be an entrepreneur but deadly if you have a job in a corporation. So I had to learn the hard way.

I wound up in publishing doing publicity and then sales, and while I learned a whole lot about the ins and outs of the publishing process and got to work with many celebrities such as Martha Stewart, George F. Will, President Jimmy Carter, and Og Mandingo, I felt like my soul was not in it. There were too many meetings, too many cover-your-ass memos to be written, lots of blame to go around, people taking credit for your ideas, and yes, the endurance of sexual harassment.

Most women my age have either been subjected to sexual harassment, know someone who has, or at the very least were not taken as seriously as men. I was listening to a news show the other day, and one of the female hosts said she used to sit around a conference table brainstorming ideas with colleagues, and frequently she would come up with an idea that was greeted negatively or with no reaction. But a few minutes later a man would say the same thing, and the reaction was "Wow! That's brilliant!" That also happened to me many times, but I didn't know other women were experiencing the same thing.

I put up with this for ten years until I finally woke up and said, "Enough! I want to start my own company." I was thirty-four years old when I quit my job to go out on my own.

Through it all my love and passion for the whole publishing process, especially working with authors, has always stayed with me. I was never happier than when one of my authors' books got on the *New York Times* bestseller list—especially if it was their first time! What a rush! Oh, the celebrations we had!

When I went out on my own as Strauss Consultants, I worked with traditional publishers as their freelance national account representative. Working on commission, I sold to large retailers and wholesalers such as Barnes & Noble, Borders (may it rest in peace), Walmart, Kmart, Priceclub Costco, and airport stores. I also found myself consulting with my clients—and they actually listened to me!

I was blessed for many years I kept a stable roster of clients and got tons of referrals—especially in the Christian publishing community! What's a nice Jewish girl from New York doing in a place like Grand Rapids?

Then Borders closed. Ebooks were invented, and Amazon disrupted the entire retail business.

I knew that if I didn't transform myself in the next few years, I wouldn't have a business.

I started working with self-publishing authors who didn't know how to sell or market their books. But it was pretty depressing when their books didn't sell. It was hard to sell books for authors who had no platform or had no idea of why they were even publishing their book. Some had successful businesses but wrote a novel because they wanted to be the next John Grisham.

It's been five years since that transition, and I have since created my own publishing company. I will be honest and say that it's been one of the most challenging things I have ever done. There have been highs and lows, personal health challenges, my father's death, and other obstacles.

I am proud to say that Hybrid Global Publishing has now published over two hundred authors, and I have a number of white label publishing brands who are working with me behind the scenes. I am proud of what I have built, and I strive to make it better each day.

After all . . . that's the Rock Star way, right?

Karen Strauss has worked in publishing for more than thirty years and has held management and marketing positions at major New York publishing houses, including Random House, Macmillan, The Free Press, Crown, and Avon. She has worked with hundreds of authors as well as New York Times *bestselling authors and celebrities such as Martha Stewart, John Grisham, Jimmy Carter, Og Mandino, Patricia Cornwall, Meg Wolitzer, Colleen McCullough, and George Will. Her publishing skills have been highly endorsed for professional quality, excellent service, and eye-catching titles and book cover designs. Many of her authors are featured in the media and at speaking engagements.*

www.hybridglobalpublishing.com

OPEN-HEARTED AND FULL OF LOVE

Shawna Swiger

Love: we want it, need it, and are surrounded by the quest for it. It's in movies, books, and magazines. Even the Beatles say that love is all we need. But when a relationship ends, it can be grueling, leaving you to vow to never love again. The demise of my marriage led me to believe that everyone should first get "divorced" before they ever enter a relationship because you will know what you want, need, and will fight for when you get it right. I'm here to tell you that you can get over that hump of pain, open your heart, and love vibrantly, passionately, and wholeheartedly.

Ask anyone and they'll agree that sometimes the end of a relationship can be the best thing that ever happens to a person. In 2009 I became a statistic, joining one out of every two marriages entering the divorce pool. It's a common tale: couple falls in and out of love, vows are broken; divorce is imminent. It was the darkest, hardest time of my life to crawl out of the wreckage that was my marriage. The legal paperwork, separating property, and preparing the house for sale were the easiest parts—all were intangibles, things that can hurt your wallet, but not your heart. Helping your child adapt to a new life of living in two households and following different rules while not changing their norm (school, friends, hobbies) was challenging. But nothing compares to rebuilding your heart.

Music served immediate help to get me through the day. "Stand" by Rascal Flatts played nearly thirty times a day during my commute, with lyrics telling me I'll dust myself off and stand up again. To truly heal from divorce requires grieving and growing that only you can do. And the grief I felt cut deep, not because I still loved him, but because I'd failed myself miserably. It was then that I realized the Beatles had gotten it wrong; love is not all we need. I'd fallen in love, and I thought it was enough. It wasn't. The more I became aware of my contributions to the disappointment that was my marriage, the more I realized that I had never determined what I wanted or needed in a relationship—I'd never looked at the basics before marrying.

Knowing what you want and need and what you will give or compromise on is critical to a successful relationship. You have to know your values and morals. Respect, honor, integrity, trust, and communication are basic requirements for a healthy relationship. Without them there will be cracks in the foundation of your bond. Recognizing that you deserve the same in return is necessary, not optional. I prayed, read books on healthy relationship practices, and surrounded myself with positive people. I went to counseling, joined a support group, and went back to church to work on my emotional and spiritual health. That's when things began to fall into place—that's when I knew what I stood for and wouldn't compromise on. I had stopped looking at the fault on the other side of the bed and had focused on my side. Forgiving both of us for our mistakes and failures brought tremendous relief, and I finally felt my heart beat again.

I changed my music and began listening to Keith Urban's "Defying Gravity" album on repeat every day for two years. I fed my mind and heart the same mantra: *I have a huge heart with a tremendous amount of love to give, and there is someone out there waiting just for me.* The album gave me hope that I could love again, that my someone was out there, and that he would find me. When doubt set in, I played the music louder so it resonated with me. I became brave enough to put myself on an online dating app with the hopes of finding love again. Though I met some nice men, I dated a few princes and many frogs. But the experience confirmed that I knew what I was looking for in a partner. And then I met my best friend.

He was kind and sweet; we clicked, realizing we had the same values, morals, and core traits, but we believed we weren't a love match. My best friend had never been married and had given up on finding her, thinking she wasn't out there. Then one late spring afternoon, he invited me to dinner. There he told me he'd been in an accident and suddenly knew he wanted to be with me; he wanted to give me everything I ever wanted, needed, and deserved in a relationship. After asking him, "Why now?" he replied, "Because when a two-thousand-pound buffalo throws you in the air, what you want in life becomes perfectly clear." It was his near-death experience that forced us to look at our relationship and what painted our truth. I was gun-shy to commit, but the more time we spent together, the more I realized he was everything I wanted and needed. Some people are fortunate to have a best friend, some are lucky to find love, but it's amazing when you fall in love with your best friend.

The darkest time in my life forced me to look at myself, commit to being the best person I can be, and know what's most important to me. I was meant to love my forever partner wholeheartedly. It takes two to make a relationship successful, and I've chosen wisely this time, as my best friend stands beside me on a strong, durable foundation. We work every day on us, committed to each other and knowing that we are our greatest investment. That's what it takes to make your relationship work: to cherish what you have and fight for it. It means putting yourself out there, letting your ego go, and truly loving all of your partner unconditionally. I'm truly thankful and joyful that my life led me exactly where I was meant to be all along: open-hearted and full of love.

Shawna Swiger is known as Your Love Gal because she cuts right to the heart of her clients' deepest love and intimacy needs and then shows them how to manifest what they want at lightning speed to reach their ultimate love, life, and relationship goals. Shawna is an energetic and inspiring tell-it-like-it-is speaker and coach who hosts coaching programs and live events every year. With over twenty-five years of conflict resolution, facilitation, and communication experience, she now shares her proven strategies for self-empowerment, confidence, and true passion with others.

www.YourLoveGal.com

JOURNEY TO NUTRITIONAL THERAPY PRACTITIONER

Bonnie Taub

Early on I realized the importance of nutrition's relationship to health. As a child I grew up in a household where my mother didn't get up to help get us ready for school. When I was in the sixth grade, a classmate fainted in class and was taken to the nurse's office. Later that day the nurse came into the classroom and gave a talk on the importance of having a well-balanced breakfast before coming to school. Apparently this student was having a cup of coffee for breakfast. When I went home that day, I asked my mother why she didn't get up to make breakfast for me and for my sister. I don't remember her answer, but I made the decision to take on that role. Besides making breakfast, I made lunches for us as well. This began my life as a "substitute mom."

By the time I was in junior high, my brother was in elementary school and twins were born, a boy and a girl. My life continued to be altered by added responsibilities. Not only was I continuing to make breakfast and lunches, but now I had to come home from school to help with the twins. My mother couldn't handle feeding, bathing, and putting two babies to bed. When they were old enough to start school, I now had four siblings to get ready for school. At this time, my mother decided to go back to school for her master's degree in library science. With this came the added responsibility of making dinner for everyone, including my father, who owned his own business and often worked late. No role model taught me how to cook. Meals were simple: meat and potatoes, canned vegetables. Breakfast was often cold cereal or Pop-Tarts. Even on weekends my mother didn't cook. Sunday morning was bagels and lox and dinner was Chinese takeout.

Even though I took a stand for what I believed in, I wasn't very independent. I was shy in school, very insecure, and afraid to answer questions in class. Luckily I did well on tests and liked to help other students. I got decent grades, so getting into college was no problem. The only problem was that I was afraid to leave home. The only good thing my parents did for me was recognizing this and refused to let me stay home. I went to a nearby school that had dorms so I stayed on campus. After a few weeks of coming home on weekends, I adjusted and only came home between semesters. This was my start on the road to independence.

After college I got married. Women in the 60s were supposed to get married and have children. Unfortunately or fortunately, children were not in the cards for me. After all, I already had raised a family. So, after a few years of marriage and tired of having to ask for every penny I wanted to spend, I went to work part time. There were some rocky times in my marriage, so I went back to school, figuring I might have to support myself someday. Through a lot of hard work on myself and in my marriage, my husband and I have a wonderful relationship and recently celebrated our fiftieth anniversary.

Going back to school helped me continue on the path to the field of holistic health. I enrolled in massage school and became a licensed massage therapist. My training included oriental medicine, where I learned to treat the whole person. This includes lifestyle and nutrition. This introduction to nutrition and the role it has on one's health led me to the Institute of Integrated Nutrition, where I became a health coach. My husband had been newly diagnosed with Crohn's disease, and I wanted desperately to help him. I learned the necessary dietary changes that helped put him into remission. To this day he continues to be healthy. It is a wonderful feeling to be able to guide someone to take control of their own healing.

My journey has also taken me into the study of lymphatic drainage and its profound effects on the health and well-being of the body. This very gentle technique can alleviate swelling and pain in muscles and joints while relaxing the body. It enhances any massage technique and shortens treatment time. I have spent many years perfecting my skills and now travel around the country as a certified teaching assistant with the Chikly Health Institute. When my husband had knee surgery, I was able to accelerate his healing while he was going through physical therapy.

The last stop on my journey happened when I found a way to combine my two passions, massage therapy and health counseling. I stumbled upon the Nutrition Therapy Association while attending a Food As Medicine conference. Their Nutrition Therapy Practitioner program teaches a unique hands-on functional evaluation: a palpating that assesses the body's needs. The client's own innate intelligence communicates to the practitioner the areas that need improvement. This could be digestion, hydration, immune function, adrenal function, or sugar imbalances. As of this writing, I have been accepted as a group leader for this year's class where I get to guide new students through their learning process. This brings me back full circle to my beginnings as a teacher.

I have been blessed in my career to find my passion in holistic health. I have my own practice where I get to do what I love. Isn't that what life is all about—being happy at what you do?

Bonnie Taub is a licensed massage therapist who graduated from the New York College of Health Professions, where she went on to the graduate program to become an AMMA Therapist and earned a bachelor's degree in Occupational Studies. As a faculty member, she taught in the massage therapy program, was a student clinic supervisor ,and therapist in the professional clinic.

Bonnie is a certified teaching assistant in the Lymph Drainage Therapy program at the Chikly Health Institute. She is also an Integrative Nutrition Health Counselor and Nutritional Therapy Practitioner. Bonnie has been in private practice since 1998.

www.yourharmonizedhealth.com